CONSCIOUS CULTURE

Thanks to the TLEX Program the connectedness and trust of the team has reached a new peak for which I am very grateful. This has resulted in a team driven for results not only for our organization but for each other.

—**Denis Piché**, Director, Public Works and Government Services Canada

Joanna Barclay has made exceptional contributions to our organization over the past couple of years. She wasted no time in impressing on our national board members the importance of having a values-driven organization when seeking to achieve high performance. As the leader of this organization, I was very receptive to the need for cultural change to help us achieve a higher level of performance, and the importance for me to lead by my actions.

—**Louis McCann**, President and CEO,
Pet Industry Joint Advisory Council, Canada

The Individual Values Assessment (IVA) I conducted with Joanna from the Barrett Values Centre was like getting an MRI for our organization. It allowed a very specific and deep-dive into the root causes of performance gaps and opportunities. Most importantly, it led to very progressive and positive changes in performance.

—**Robert Francis Seguin**, Managing Partner,
The Productive Leadership Institute

Joanna was integral in transforming my client engagement network from a loose committee to strong leadership team. This was achieved through the use of the Barrett Cultural Transformation Tools. But the best tool of all was Joanna herself.

—**Daniel Leclair**, Director General,
Public Works and Government Services Canada

I was mandated by the Chelsea Foundation Board to lead efforts to establish a strategic planning process to equip our organization with the culture and tools to attain aspired results. I was recommended Joanna Barclay and have not regretted it! Joanna is a true professional and very passionate about facilitating cultural change and strategic planning. She is a joy to work with and you always feel totally supported in your efforts. An excellent facilitator, mentor and coach, she is calm, focused and caring and has kept us on track.

—**Enrico Valente**, President at TIFOSI Motorsports Club

Although our employee engagement is above 85%, our Leadership Team felt strongly about ensuring that our culture would be able to manage ongoing change. With that in mind, our work with Joanna, through the use of the Barrett Cultural Transformational Tools has not only given us the data that we needed to ensure that our current and desired cultural values were well defined, but also a plan to address how to get to the desired set of values. Thank you Joanna!

—**Michael J. Tremblay**
President, Astellas Pharma Canada, Inc.

Cultural transformation is an important issue and one that can bring about results, high performance, and excellence as well as quality experiences for people to overcome the disconnection, alienation and "suffering" that plagues our current organizational world. Both Joanna and the program are excellent. The content is so unique and integrative.

—**Rhonda St. Croix**, Office of Education, Change Consultant
Royal College of Physicians and Surgeons of Canada

Joanna, your masterful facilitation has been instrumental to our group accomplishing the vision. Thank you for your determination, dedication, vision, teaching, patience, time and love for us and the Art of Living.

—**Debra Joy Eklove**, President, Art of Living Foundation, Canada

Only when your culture is conscious can you manage it, and that is exactly what this book enables you to do.

—**Richard Barrett**, Chairman and Founder of the Barrett Values Centre

CONSCIOUS CULTURE

*How to Build a High Performing
Workplace through Values,
Ethics, and Leadership*

JOANNA
BARCLAY

NEW YORK

CONSCIOUS CULTURE
How to Build a High Performing Workplace
through Values, Ethics, and Leadership

© 2015 Joanna Barclay.

Published in New York, New York, by Morgan James Publishing. Morgan James and The Entrepreneurial Publisher are trademarks of Morgan James, LLC. www.MorganJamesPublishing.com

The Morgan James Speakers Group can bring authors to your live event. For more information or to book an event visit The Morgan James Speakers Group at www.TheMorganJamesSpeakersGroup.com.

A **free** eBook edition is available with the purchase of this print book.

CLEARLY PRINT YOUR NAME ABOVE IN UPPER CASE

Instructions to claim your free eBook edition:
1. Download the BitLit app for Android or iOS
2. Write your name in **UPPER CASE** on the line
3. Use the BitLit app to submit a photo
4. Download your eBook to any device

ISBN 978-1-63047-153-8 paperback
ISBN 978-1-63047-154-5 eBook
ISBN 978-1-63047-155-2 hardcover
Library of Congress Control Number: 2014934763

Cover Design by:
Rachel Lopez
www.r2cdesign.com

Interior Design by:
Bonnie Bushman
bonnie@caboodlegraphics.com

In an effort to support local communities, raise awareness and funds, Morgan James Publishing donates a percentage of all book sales for the life of each book to Habitat for Humanity Peninsula and Greater Williamsburg.

Get involved today, visit
www.MorganJamesBuilds.com

Habitat
for Humanity®
Peninsula and
Greater Williamsburg
Building Partner

For my husband, Tom, and children, Stephanie, Lorne, and Bobby.
Thank you for your love, devotion, and commitment.
You continue to be my inspiration.

In memory of
Nelson Mandela: July 18, 1918 – December 5, 2014

Nelson Mandela was an inspiration to leaders across the world of the life force in human values.

His courage to forgive and compassion for all earned him the respect and trust necessary to unite a nation.

May we find equal courage to unite in solving our global challenges.

"During my lifetime I have dedicated myself to this struggle of the African people. I have fought against white domination, and I have fought against black domination. I have cherished the ideal of a democratic and free society in which all persons live together in harmony and with equal opportunities. It is an ideal which I hope to live for and to achieve. But if need be, it is an ideal for which I am prepared to die."
April 20, 1964

Table of Contents

Figures, Tables, Worksheets and Case Studies

Figures

Tables

Worksheets

Case Studies

Shantih Mantra

Let us be together.
Let us enjoy the whole world and this life together.
Let us grow in strength together.
Let us become effulgent and shine together.
Let us not hate each other.
Let there be peace in our soul, mind and environment.

—Katha Upanishad

Introduction

World Forum for Ethics in Business

Talk by **H. H. Sri Sri Ravi Shankar**,
Geneva, Switzerland, July 1, 2013

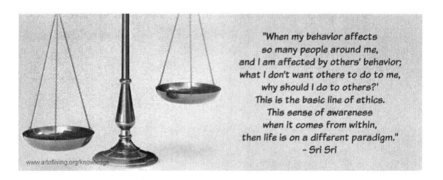

"When my behavior affects so many people around me, and I am affected by others' behavior; what I don't want others to do to me, why should I do to others?' This is the basic line of ethics. This sense of awareness when it comes from within, then life is on a different paradigm."
- Sri Sri

www.artofliving.org/knowledge

Your Excellency, and my dear ones and the audience. Crisis brings out the best and the worst in people.

When the recent Himalayas tsunami happened, I didn't tell any of the volunteers to go and do something. Without me telling anyone, there were already thousands of volunteers who just plunged into various activities. I would say this is real ethics, the feeling that comes from your heart.

When we inculcate this in the educational system, bring attention and awareness of one's attitude and behavior, we find a sea of change in our society.

Just a week ago, there was a crisis in India. During this crisis, there were people who plunged in to save others and there were some who exploited even for a glass of water.

It is in these moments of crisis that we can gauge ethics, whether it is genuine or cosmetic.

Ethics cannot be cosmetic, it has to come out in a genuine manner. Now, how does one bring about genuine ethics in people, or make a person feel that one has to really be ethical.

I just want to narrate an incident. There is a corrupt person working in a bank, he is a trouble-maker and he does not listen to anybody. I asked them to send him to me, so I could have a word with him.

I told this gentleman, "Would you like your driver to be honest with you or cheat you?"

He replied, "I don't like my driver to cheat me, it is obvious."

Then I asked him, "Would you appreciate it if a colleague is cheating on you?"

He said, "No, I don't want my colleague or friend to cheat on me."

I said, "Look, you don't want your boss to be dishonest with you. You don't want your subordinate to be dishonest with you. You don't want your colleague to be dishonest with you. You expect honesty from everyone, sincerity from everybody; how about you?"

That suddenly made him sit back and think, "Yes, I don't even want my maid servant at home to cheat on me, I don't want my driver to cheat on me, I don't want my colleague on whom I have to rely on to cheat on me; then why would I cheat on someone else?"

He had never thought about it like this before; it made him think, re-think!

"When my behavior affects so many people around me, and I am affected by others' behavior; what I don't want others to do to me, why should I do to others?"

This is the basic line of ethics. This sense of awareness when it comes from within, then life is on a different paradigm. There is a very visible shift.

If you have ever been to a prison anytime, I mean just to take a look at it; if you had a word or two with people in the prison, you would see that they are good people. These people who are condemned as criminals, there is a good person hiding inside them, there is an ethical and compassionate person hiding inside them too. That personality needs to come out, blossom and flower.

When I visited prisons, I spoke to thousands of inmates. They said they committed the crime in a moment of an emotional upsurge, when they were not in control, and then they regretted it.

How can we help these people who are corrupt and involved in criminal activities? I think it is possible. If we can educate them on how they can handle their own mind and their emotions then that would bring a big change.

They say, "Neither at school nor at home has a broader vision about life been given to us. Nobody ever told us to attend to our emotions our minds."

A sense of inner cleansing can bring about ethics.

Stress and violent tendencies in an individual need to be checked. I am sure if these tendencies are checked, and if people are given tools or counseled to get over these tendencies which they have acquired either due to ignorance or through difficult family situations, we can bring about the best of ethics from within them.

If those in correctional houses can be transformed, I am sure the common man can realize and live those ethics in their day-to-day life; it is not so difficult. I don't find any reason for us to not believe in a more ethical and compassionate society for the coming generation. Of course, the present situation looks very bleak; we see crime and violence everywhere.

In the last year in America alone, there were 10 million acts of crime and violence recorded. If you go throughout the world, we have 7 billion people; I am sure there are a few billion acts of violence that are happening in the society. I feel it is high time we put our attention towards bringing back ethics, not just in business, but in social and civic society.

There are four pillars of our society and we need to attend to all four pillars—politics, business, faith-based organizations, and civil society. Unless ethics percolates in all four different areas of our human society, we cannot find the most desired transformation happening.

Once again, I will reinstate the point that ethics need to be inculcated, cultivated and nurtured. The seed is already present in every human being, it is already there, it just needs a little more nurturing—in politics, business, faith-based organizations, and also in civic society. If all these four institutions work together, we can definitely make a difference in this coming century.

With these few words, I congratulate the organizers, and all of you who have come here to deliberate on this very important topic of today's Ethics in Business. Thank you very much.

Keynote talk by — *H. H. Sri Sri Ravi Shankar*

Acknowledgements

Thank you to my husband, Tom Barclay, for his never-ending support and love. This book could not have been written if it wasn't for the space and time he gave me to write it. His presence in my life is truly a blessing. To my son, Bobby, for being there day to day during the creative writing process, and helping with the organization and execution challenges by adapting his culinary skills in the kitchen.

Sincere thanks to Bob Urichuck, sales guru extraordinaire, for his encouragement to share my experience and knowledge. He was a never-ending supply of energy and confidence, graciously sharing his experience as a speaker, writer, and trainer.

Special thanks to Carol Kline for her workshop and coaching on *Write Your Transformational Best Seller.* Her experience, knowledge, and ability to demystify the writing and publishing process was extremely valuable.

Many heartfelt thanks to Richard Barrett, Phil Clothier, Mary Jane Bullen, the Barrett Values Centre (BVC) team, and the global BVC consultants who live the philosophy of abundance and graciously share their knowledge and resources.

A big thank-you to Bill Staples, Duncan Holmes, Jo Nelson, Wayne Nelson, John Miller, and the ICA Associates of Canada for sharing the precious gifts in the Technology of Participation (ToP®) methodology and ToP® resources that empower leaders in creating a culture of participation.

To my editor, Karen Runtz, an enormous thank-you for her patience and attention to detail. Her experience and professionalism was highly treasured. I am very grateful to all the friends and associates who gave their precious time to review the chapters and provide valuable feedback.

To the TLEX Team past and present, Michael Fischman, John Osborne, Christoph Glazer, Rajita Kulkarni, Johann Berlin, Mandar Apte, Debra Eklove, Spencer Delisle, Madhuri Karode, and Susannah Rowley, thank you for your dedication and devotion in sharing the wisdom of Sri Sri Ravi Shankar. Your service is making a difference in the world and contributing to transformation in society.

To my teacher, Sri Sri Ravi Shankar, I feel honored and blessed to be the vehicle through which the knowledge in this book has been shared. With the deepest gratitude, thank you.

Jai Guru Dev
Much love,
Joanna Barclay

Servant Leadership Background

"The Purpose of Life is a Life of Purpose"

When reading this book, my British/Finnish son-in-law, Nicholas Burton, asked me to share the following advice with you: to "read between the lines" and keep in mind your culture and the differences that exist between yourself and the author.

Born and raised in Canada into a military family, I was number four of five children. My father, Robert Fletcher, who was British, decided to transfer to the Canadian military after marrying my mother, a Canadian, in Berlin after the Second World War. His reason for the transfer was that he believed the Canadian army to be "family friendly" with regard to postings, a way of life in the military. It's just as well. Our family ended up moving thirteen times before I graduated from high school.

My mother, Simonne Fletcher, was the daughter of a three-star general in the Canadian army, General Maurice Pope, who, after retiring from the military, became a two-time Ambassador for Canada to Spain and Belgium. His father, my great-grandfather, Sir Joseph Pope, was knighted for his public service to the Canadian government, and his father's sister, my great-aunt, Georgina Pope, was the first Canadian to receive the Canadian Red Cross, for her service during the Boer War in South Africa. Their father, my great-great-grandfather, William Henry Pope, was a Father of Confederation for

Prince Edward Island and instrumental in facilitating Canada's birth as a confederated nation.

If servant leadership is in the genes, I would tend to agree based on the professions I have chosen in life.

It is said that the two most important days of your life are the day you are born and no, not the day you die, but the day you realize why you are born. Why is the second so important? Because discovering your true purpose or calling in life connects to your inner passion for living. How you see the world, the decisions you make to earn a living and what you do from then on is influenced by an inner desire to grow and fulfill your life's purpose.

In 2000, I changed professional careers and became a Certified Professional Facilitator when I discovered my true purpose after taking a group facilitation course with the Institute of Cultural Affairs. The most profound awakening took place. There was a deep inner knowing that this was the work I was born to fulfill. Now, every time I facilitate, it's in the role of servant leadership, helping leaders create a culture of participation by developing collaborative connections, increasing team synergy, and building consensus. Being a facilitative leader gives me the opportunity to facilitate change by the people, for the people, and help them reach their true potential.

A course I took through the Art of Living Foundation in 2003 brought a new dimension to life as I discovered the benefits of yoga and meditation for personal and professional development. Recognizing the power of the tools and techniques taught on the course and how they develop the full potential of individuals, I decided I wanted to give back to society and make a difference in people's lives by becoming a teacher for the Foundation, an international educational and humanitarian organization. I continue to fulfill this mission and purpose in my current position as Canadian Director of the TLEX Program, delivered by the International Association of Human Values, the sister foundation of the Art of Living.

By far the most meaningful of all roles in my life has been that of a loving mother and wife. Along with my husband, our three children are a constant source of love, inspiration, and growth.

The greatest wish I have for this book is that it leads to an awakening of human values, ethics, and leadership that serves to transform business results to unite us in working together for the betterment of society.

Preface

Creativity and inspiration tend to strike at the most unusual times. It happened to me the morning of my first webinar on "Building a High Performing Culture." I awoke at 3:30 a.m. and jumped out of bed with a new "AH HA!" My subconscious had been working while I slept and connected many truths about values and performance. The realization seemed obvious yet so easy to miss. I experienced a feeling of euphoria that was so intense I couldn't keep from leaping around the bedroom. The discovery could have such significant impact for organizational leaders—something they are on the lookout for to inspire and motivate their people and create high performing workplaces.

What hit me that morning was a source of life force energy that everyone everywhere could benefit from. That source is our personal values.

Personal values are a source of life force energy. They energize us, make us feel happy, give us joy when they are lived and sorrow or frustration when they are not. They are the embodiment of our heart and soul calling us to action, connecting us to the world around us, and helping us perform to our highest potential.

For leaders, values are the heartbeat of excellence that intrinsically motivate and inspire their people. For managers, these are the things they want to make sure are frequently acknowledged and recognized. The more a person is aware of their values the more valuable the values become for them and the world around them. Awakening your personal values is a source of inspiration and motivation, a source of high performance that comes from within. For example, I value continuous learning. Continuous learning is important to me because it enables personal growth and development, and increases my self-esteem and sense of self-worth. Feeling more competent and capable adds value and purpose to my life.

Values seem so simple and yet they are so profound. How many people are aware of the values in life that motivate them and give them extra energy? How often do people let others know what it is that will drive them to give 110% on the job and in life?

Like the air we breathe, our lives without values would be empty, lifeless, and soulless. Our personal values are at the core of who we are, what we believe in, our self-worth, and how we behave. When we are living our personal values we feel good, we have a positive mental attitude, and feel like we are living life to the fullest.

To truly appreciate the power of personal values, think of a time when you were in conflict with someone, when your values were stepped on because what you valued was being ignored. How did it feel? Imagine your highest value is trust. Your manager tells you that the project you have been promised for six months is going to be given to another person. Irrespective of the reasons why, how would you feel—angry, frustrated, let down? When the values that define who you are at the core of your being are ignored or disrespected, the feeling can be intensely negative. You feel your self-worth is being threatened. You may feel so uncomfortable the emotions cause you to want to leave that team or organization.

Treat a person right and you have a loyal friend for life. Mistreat them by stepping on their values and you have one very unhappy, potentially dangerous individual.

Our values are a source of personal excellence and high performance. They exist inside of us all the time. All we need to do is awaken them. Removing stress at a deep level in the human system is one way. Stress can inhibit self-awareness—some people bury their emotions as a self-protection mechanism. Once the stress is removed, a person's sense of perception becomes clearer and they are better able to observe their thoughts and emotions. Another way is to make the time for personal reflection to discover their values. Who am

I? What gives me joy and happiness? What means the most to me and why? What do I do when I am living these values?

Today I might answer creativity, teamwork, and freedom. When I am able to live these values my spirit soars and I produce my best results.

Imagine the power a conscious leader would have if they knew how to unleash the unlimited power of values within their organization. Conscious leaders are able to integrate the head and the heart by developing self-awareness and emotional intelligence, while empowering others to do the same. The possibilities and opportunities are endless. Some of the most successful companies have figured it out and invest in their culture for this reason.

Look at Google, Ikea, Southwest Airlines, and Amazon, a few of the most successful corporations in America. Each one of these firms is at least 1649% more profitable for investors over a 15-year period.[1] This begs the question, how do they do it? The answer is they invest in their culture and consider it to be one of their most valuable assets. They have learned which values and behaviors mean the most to their stakeholders, and enliven those values in everything they do and every decision they make. An example of this is Google, which hires three-star chefs in all of their campuses and provides gourmet meals 24x7. One financial impact of this culture is they do not have to search for talent. The top talent is lined up at Google's door wanting to join the team, contribute, and make a difference.

Culture can be defined as how you do things, your management style, and the way you make decisions. The way you do things is heavily dependent on your values and norms of behavior. Are you an inspirational leader? Do you lead by example? Or is command and control more your comfort zone where you expect people to "do as I say and not as I do?" In today's business world values are playing a much greater role in strategic decision making and are now a topic of discussion around the boardroom table. Why? Because values such as integrity, loyalty, respect, and trust are key drivers for financial success: they are directly connected to how you implement your vision and strategies, and the personality of the people, in particular the leadership. The organizational culture you create will enable you to attract, retain, and draw out the best talent available to you. Recent studies show that the number one reason why nine out of ten strategic

1   Raj Sisodia; Conscious Capitalism, 2013 (publisher, etc needed, APA rules)

initiatives fail is a disregard for an organization's existing culture and the effort it takes to change behavior[2].

There is a well-known saying by Peter Drucker: *"Culture eats strategy for breakfast."* Applied to culture change this means whatever new strategies a leadership team creates will not succeed unless they are aligned with the current or desired culture. How can you expect different results unless you focus consciously on changing the way people behave and interact with each other?

Leadership is recognizing how important empowered employees, collaboration, and the power of collective action are to achieving business results. The ability to achieve internal cohesion on decisions is valued and is now becoming the goal. This is a shift in thinking and behavior from "me" to "we". The "we" is the ability to create shared goals with shared values. Having a common approach to achieving the goals is the new way of working together. Imagine what this will mean to leaders who only know a command and control style of leadership. It will require the development of a new leadership style— one that is more facilitative with a focus on building consensus and engaging participation. This can be a huge change in what leaders' value, the way they behave and how performance is measured. The way of reaching your goals and realizing your strategies is embedded in how people act and interact with one another. We all know Einstein's theory of insanity: "doing the same things over and over again and expecting different results." Well here's mine for cultural insanity: *Expecting your employees to embrace new work habits and higher levels of collaboration between teams, while maintaining the same management style, organizational values, and behaviors.*

In the current global climate where increasing awareness and knowledge management is a competitive advantage, it would stand to reason that creating a conscious culture would be a management priority. This begs the question: *"Are you thinking about investing in your culture or will you continue to have an unconscious, default culture?"*

There are several reasons to invest in creating a conscious culture:

• To become an employer of choice, and build a high performing workplace.

---

2   What Drives Strategy Implementation? Top Line Findings (2009) Bridges Business Consultancy Int.

- To increase employee engagement and retention.
- To build a new culture after a merger or acquisition.
- To conduct an environmental scan prior to strategic planning.

The aim of this book is to demonstrate the power that values, ethics and transformational leadership have to transform your business and build a high performing culture. Having been involved in corporate transformations for the past thirty years and being a facilitative leader for half that time, I would like to share wisdom and experience to help your transformation journey. The ideas are aimed at making a difference for the people in or associated with your organization: your employees, clients, suppliers, and the communities in which you operate.

Building a high performing culture entails transformation, both personal and organizational. This can take between two to five years because new consciousness is developed and emerges over time. The challenges with all forms of transformation are the feelings of uncertainty and fear that arise when letting go of something known, and being in a state of flux or transition on unsolid ground, journeying towards an end point you do not know. Transformation is uncomfortable and stressful, and these feelings will likely persist until a new, more permanent end state emerges. This is why understanding and managing the human dynamics of change is so important and why no one likes change if they are not in control of it.

The title of this book could also have read *What CEOs need to know about culture to…*

- Transform personal excellence into organizational excellence
- Generate greater engagement and productivity
- Manage the human dynamics of effective change

These are just a few of the benefits in building a conscious corporate culture. **The first objective of this book is to show how transformational leadership can address three major challenges for employees: engagement, retention, and burnout.**

There's nothing worse for an employee than not wanting to come in to work in the morning. I believe the end goal for all leaders is having a "WOW" culture, where people can be at their best and bring their full selves to work, where they love what they do. In this kind of engaged environment, retention, and burnout cease to be an issue because employees are energized and passionate about their work. This kind of positive mental attitude is a natural state of peak performance. To achieve it often requires dedication to personal development and self-mastery. These can be developed through programs such as the Transformational Leadership for Excellence (TLEX), in chapter 7 under *Tools for Inner and Outer Transformation*.

In today's society, change has become the new norm. Many people complain about how this constant state of change is draining their energy levels and performance. The reality is we are managing change all the time. We change our hair styles, clothing, the food we eat, our cars, homes, on a regular basis. Change is good when we have control over it—when we want it and actively participate in making the decisions.

The problems with change arise when it is being "done to" us and we do not feel we have an "active part" in the change process. The feeling of being "done to" is stressful and has a draining effect on an individual's performance and organizational effectiveness. No one wants to feel "done to" in life. For this reason the whole change process improves when it is collaborative and leaders invite as much participation as possible.

Transformational leadership is transformative. It moves an organization from being focused on "me" (self-interest) to being focused on "we" (common good). Facilitative leaders unify the organization and bring out the best in people. When transformational leaders are facilitative, employees come alive. This happens when leaders focus their attention on others and invite employees to participate, seek their advice, work as a team and build consensus. The art and science of transformational facilitative leadership is the ability to connect the hearts and minds of people. It empowers group members to share perspectives and learn from each other. In the process, this increases self-awareness and awareness of others. It accesses the wisdom of the group and creates sustainable solutions with high impact. Being engaged and empowered in this way builds commitment for decision making and the ability to take new actions and behaviors that support the transformation process.

The second objective of this book is to share strategies and processes for continuous improvement that will enable leaders to measure, map and manage cultural transformation.

Cultural transformation happens over time. Being able to measure annual progress is vital for continuous learning, continuous improvement, and course correction. Each year a new focus can be identified along with specific initiatives to support the changes. It's like a marriage. How many people have been in a relationship where you wanted to change your partner? How successful were you in the first year? The second year? The third year? Changing culture is similar. It is about transforming people's mindsets, beliefs, values, and behaviors. When done successfully this kind of transformation happens gradually over a period of time, usually several years.

Many transformations fail to have the impact that leaders are looking for. The major reason is the difficulty in *ensuring that staff members take different actions or demonstrate new behaviors.* This is about changing culture, changing the way things are done in the organization—a shift that is not adequately addressed or managed.

Perhaps you've heard the saying: "*The soft stuff is the hard stuff.*" Changing the way people behave is hard stuff. We are complex; we have emotions, values, and beliefs that make us unique. These elements are hard to work with because they are underneath the surface and we can't see them. Have you ever found it hard trying to figure out why your partner is upset? Wouldn't it be nice if a sign flashed above their head saying "You're stepping on my values, the things I care for most in the whole wide world?" Then at least you would know why they are upset and could act appropriately to make them feel better.

Transpose this to an organization that is going through change. Imagine all the different value sets you are working with. Wouldn't it be nice to have tools that help you identify the values under the surface that motivate human behavior and the values staff would like to experience so they can feel fully engaged and respected?

Cultural transformation tools help you assess intangible values and behaviors. They make the intangible-tangible, and allow you to measure progress on a regular basis. A baseline measurement helps management to see the progress and most importantly, to communicate the same throughout the organization, to create conscious awareness and competence.

The third objective of this book is to reveal how personal values are a source of inspiration, energy, and positive mental attitude.

The law of performance states: Ability x Mental Attitude = Performance.

When our mental attitude is low or zero, guess what kind of performance we have? All the ability in the world (knowledge, experience, training, education, etc.) will not help you perform better when your mental attitude is disengaged and negative.

Leaders get excited when they figure out ways to increase intrinsic personal motivation for their employees. Why? Because external means of increasing motivation are having less impact and are being reduced in times of economic restraint.

So how do you increase personal motivation? How do you engage staff and increase their sense of personal fulfillment and performance?

There is a simple and very powerful way: ask them what they value most on the job and in the workplace.

Everyone I have asked in my seminars and workshops recognizes the leap in performance they have when they are able to experience what they value most—and, conversely, the harmful impact when their values are ignored or disrespected. In fact, they would not want to continue working for the organization, and many have said they left jobs because of misalignment in values.

As leaders we often think we have to hide our emotions and values as they make us vulnerable. Doing so negates the power of emotional intelligence. Your empathy, compassion, and caring for individuals will raise your esteem in the eyes of staff far more than being autocratic and controlling. When people know how much you care, then they care how much you know. They will listen and follow your leadership because caring builds a sense of belonging, trust, and trustworthiness. Have you ever listened and given your commitment to someone you didn't trust?

Our personal values are an incredible, untapped resource because most of us are unaware of what they are. We don't make the time for self-reflection and we certainly don't discuss them in a group setting to see how they can be connected for the benefit of the team. In life, human values are the one thing that connects us and empowers each one of us.

Most of us get up in the morning wanting to do good, be our best, make a difference in the world, and add value to life. This enlivens us and makes us feel good. When we feel good we have a positive mental attitude.

Can our values change and transform over time? Certainly. Our own consciousness or awareness is the tool and the object of change. When I am aware or conscious of something, change can happen. If I am not aware, things continue as they were.

What new thing have you discovered today? To become more conscious, it helps to have an inquisitive mind, being open to information, positive or negative, without personalizing or seeking to blame. These mindsets allow new thoughts, ideas, and possibilities to emerge. Expanding our consciousness is a way to access creative, innovative ideas that have not been thought of before. Such ideas empower and enable personal and corporate transformation.

If you are looking for new ways to increase the effectiveness of your team or organization, start by identifying the personal values that mean the most to people. Find out what they are currently experiencing both positive and limiting and what they would like to be experiencing instead to make work meaningful. Then carry out two to three actions to show that you heard and are actively listening.

And watch the impact on your team's performance!

Part 1

Building a Values-Driven Organization

The first part of the book sets the stage for the power and energy of values—how values, when consciously lived in the work environment, fuel high performance and sustainable growth.

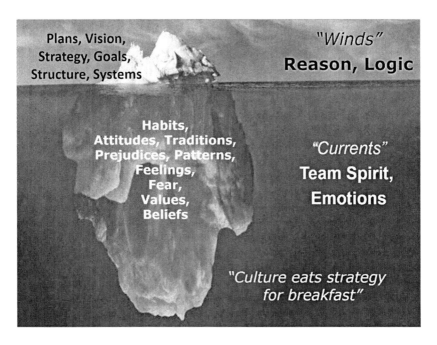

Figure Part 1 – Culture Eats Strategy for Breakfast

Chapter 1

The ABCs of High Performance

All power and effectiveness comes from knowing how things happen and acting accordingly.

—Tao of Leadership

I magine knowing the "how" to all your problems. Wouldn't life be so much simpler? No more sleepless nights worrying about staff reactions to decisions, or how you are going to reach your target goals, or how your systems and processes are going to be able to manage the workload.

Knowing the how, consciously or unconsciously, is like having a blueprint to everything you need to do. The three forces for generating this power are awareness, belongingness, and commitment.

Awareness through Measurement

Awareness through measurement creates new consciousness. When we measure things we are provided with data to make sense of the world around us. Data and information answer our questions about why, what, and how. New information creates new awareness and we become more conscious of what is happening and why. Performance measurement systems are designed for this purpose. Systems like the Balanced Score Card (Kaplan and Norton 1993, 1996, 2001), or the TPM Process (Jones and Schilling 2000) or Performance Prism (Neely 2002) are all useful for helping leaders measure and manage the performance of their organizations.

There is no one-size-fits-all way of measuring performance because organizational structures are diverse and business requirements are unique.

New consciousness is the source of new ideas. New ideas are the source of new strategies. New strategies are the source of new actions to solve problems or capitalize on opportunities. New actions give you a measureable way to manage change. What you measure you can manage. Knowing the how leads to appropriate actions.

Knowing what is happening in the organization is the first step down the road to success. When I think about organizational performance, the image of an iceberg comes to mind. I like this metaphor because it captures powerful elements that are happening both above and below the surface. Above the water leaders are responsible for creating the vision, strategizing, and planning. Leaders are happiest working above the surface where it is rational and tangible, using skills at which they excel. Decisions are based on fact and reasoning according to the winds of change happening externally in the marketplace or the world around them.

The managers and employees responsible for fulfilling the mission and purpose of the organization are below the water, focused on the operations and efficient functioning of systems and processes. This is why knowing the "how" is so important. The cultural element is beneath the surface, made up of the organization's habits, traditions, attitudes, prejudices, patterns, feelings, beliefs, and values. Sometimes considered intangible and difficult to see, they have a huge impact on how things get done.

What sunk the *Titanic* was not above the waterline but below. The currents of emotions within an organization are at play beneath the surface. The saying,

"Culture eats strategy for breakfast," is an apt description of the power of cultural currents and their impact on strategic initiatives. How people do things, the management style, and the way decisions are made all play out here. Beneath the surface is where habits and traditions exist that either engage and empower people or hold them back from wanting to adapt to change. Here is where attitudes and beliefs stirring prejudice exist, and where values and behaviors are expressed and lived.

If I wanted to move the iceberg where would I apply pressure to have the most impact? Pushing on the peak above the waterline would make it wobble and tip over. However, if I apply pressure under the surface it would move the mass forward. The same holds true for organizations. What drives performance is not what is above the surface but what is beneath the surface: the currents of emotions, the team spirit, and the culture. By learning how to work successfully with the culture and team spirit, you will be able to carry out the vision, strategies, and plans in response to the market demands and opportunities.

Another good metaphor is that of a garden. It is the quality of the soil beneath the surface that makes a garden gain color, grow and flourish. Like a gardener in the garden, the leader needs to nurture the soil and make sure the roots are getting all the nutrients they need to be strong, grounded and healthy. The well-being of the garden depends on the condition of the roots.

Figure 1-1 — Tree of Life

In the movie *Avatar* we see scientists experimenting and learning about the interconnecting life force that permeates the forest's root system. We are told this root system is responsible for distributing a natural intelligence. As part of nature, we too have a root system, a natural energy that connects us to each other. This energy radiates from our hearts.[3] The science and study of contextual cardiology has demonstrated the existence and power of the heart's energy.[4] The heart is a source of emotional intelligence and intuition. The more we practice connecting to our heart's energy and emotional intelligence, the wiser and more effective we will become in leading ourselves and leading others.

The challenge with culture is how does a leader manage to measure the intangible elements beneath the surface? It is very difficult to measure values, fears, or beliefs. Yet when it comes to change, these are the very things that will have the greatest impact on your success.

How does a leader inspire trust in people to willingly let go of traditions and attitudes that have supported and protected them? How does a leader discern the level of emotional uncertainty and fear in letting go of processes that brought them success or the need to learn new techniques that will take a while to master? How willing are they to change their mindset, what they value, along with the associated behaviors?

Culture eats strategy for breakfast because it is far more difficult to change culture than it is to develop a strategy and to see it carried out. The success rate of strategy implementation depends a great deal on the strategy's alignment with the current culture of the organization. Any strategy that entails a change in culture will surely run into a roadblock as tight as Fort Knox. What makes cultural transformation so difficult? It is the connection of values and behaviors to people's sense of identity and security. This is what the ego knows. Try and change what the ego is comfortable with and immediately alarm bells go off inside people. Change in values and behaviors means a change in the emotional makeup of a person. If I define my success by my relationships and how well I manage my people, and you ask me to take over the management of a new team from a function I know nothing about, how comfortable and willing to adapt to change do you think I'm going to be?

3   Institute of Heartmath: http://www.heartmath.org/
4   Contextual cardiology: http://www.ccjm.org/content/74/Suppl_1/S99.full.pdf+html

We don't like change unless it is something we personally want to do. We gladly accept a new golf club or a new hair cut because we know this is something that will make us feel or look better. Ask a person to trust and collaborate and work as a team with a colleague they previously competed with; that is a different story. The emotions associated with values and behaviors go deep into the fiber and makeup of a person. They are what define a personality and inspire and motivate performance. Asking a person to change their values is like asking a leopard to change its spots overnight. Not possible. If you have a partner or spouse, have they ever tried to change you? How successful were they?

People eventually surrender or leave a relationship if their values are continually ignored or stepped on. In our North American culture most people have the freedom and financial means to leave a relationship if it is not meeting their emotional needs. It is the same in an organization. People leave because their values and strengths are not recognized or because the work is performed in a way that is contrary to their beliefs and how they were trained. Engagement and retention are directly connected to people's values. Values are a source of life force energy and fuel high performance. If they cannot be lived there will be negative consequences such as disengagement. If they can be lived, the opposite is true. Creativity, teamwork, productivity, and engagement will drive high performance.

Many organizations are living in misery and doing nothing about their problems. Yet when we know there is something wrong and we ask for guidance, the answer is a gift. Knowledge is power. It makes you happy and increases your intelligence and consciousness. When new information is gathered through a values assessment or stakeholder consultations, leaders and employees become empowered with ideas and creativity to act and make a difference.

You learn which values are important to people and what they are currently experiencing, both the positive strengths and limiting behaviors. People share what they would like to see happening, providing a roadmap to successful change.

New awareness brings emotional support and intellectual clarity. Education and knowledge increase your levels of consciousness. By measuring your current culture, leaders find out which values are most important to their people. With this knowledge leaders are able to make more meaningful emotional connections. This connection creates a sense of belongingness and internal cohesion, strengthening and uniting the organization, increasing its adaptability in times of change.

If I were to ask you to describe the new style of leadership that is emerging in organizations with the most attractive, efficient, high performing work environments, what qualities would you see? How about respectful, caring, enthusiastic, honest, good communicator, collaborative, committed, accountable, helpful, coach, excellence, trustworthy, integrity, ethical, and visionary? Notice that most of these qualities are "soft" as opposed to "hard" leadership disciplines. If you were an employee and you worked for a leader with these qualities, how would they make you feel? Perhaps you would feel valued, respected, loyal, enthusiastic, positive, happy, energized, committed, engaged, and empowered. Notice how reciprocal these values are. What you give you receive. Now observe the energy in these feelings and how they might drive personal performance. Visualize the impact it would have on achieving results if you could harness this energy and use it to create a workplace where people are thriving, excited to come to work, and giving their 100%. This is a high performing culture.

The opposite reciprocating effect is also present when negative leadership qualities are experienced in the work environment. What would it feel like to work for a leader who was disrespectful, dishonest, authoritative, demanding, and manipulative? I can imagine it would be stressful, drain the life force out of you on a daily basis, cause disengagement and reduced productivity.

The journey of cultural transformation begins with awareness—self-awareness, awareness of others and what is happening around you. A paradigm shift is taking place in leadership as the baby boomers are leaving organizations and being replaced by younger leaders who were raised with a different set of values, education, and living conditions. Leaders are recognizing the importance of "soft" skills, such as empathy and heart-to-heart communication, the power they have in developing trust relationships, and the self-mastery it takes to develop them. How aware am I of my leadership values? How does my behavior affect others? Am I a joy to work for? The answers to these questions will help you be a more effective leader. Tools such as the Leadership Values Assessment (a 360 tool) help leaders tune in to their values and behaviors, and how they are influencing the work environment. Reference table 8-2 in Chapter 8.

"Organizational transformation begins with the personal transformation of the leaders. Organizations don't change. People do!"[5] Leaders who "own" their values and lead accordingly develop stronger trust relationships with staff that gives rise to high productivity.

With a desire for greater self-awareness, awareness about others and what is happening around you, you are showing others you care about them. This creates a sense of belongingness and team connectedness. The saying "People don't care how much you know until they know how much you care" is a powerful statement to live by in leading people through change. Feeling cared for creates a sense of belongingness and inner connection in people. With awareness and belongingness comes trust and commitment. Altogether, awareness, belongingness, and commitment generate the organizational strength to tackle challenges together and achieve amazing results.

With increased self-mastery, leaders are more aware of the need for greater vulnerability and authenticity and the importance their values play in determining their leadership style. A true values-based leader driving phenomenal organizational performance consciously operates from both the head and the heart. Feeling connected to staff on an emotional level is a key motivator and influencer for creating attractive, efficient work environments where people are fully engaged intellectually and emotionally.

When we leave for the office in the morning we bring our emotions with us; we don't leave them at home. Why then do leaders park them in the parking lot and hold back their feelings and values when communicating with staff? What makes leaders feel vulnerable and prefer not to share their emotions? What are they afraid of? The old model of leadership was primarily rational, left-brained and analytical. Not any longer. Emotions like trust, compassion, and loyalty are being discussed around the boardroom table because loyalty is an emotion connected to the heart not the brain.

There is life force energy in our hearts that speaks and expresses itself in the world through our personal values and behaviors. This energy drives our behavior and fuels our performance. We feel energized when we are performing and doing the things we love, value, and believe in. I value teamwork. If I'm working on a project for the team, I will work until all hours in the night to complete the

---

5   Liberating the Corporate Soul, *Building a Visionary Organization,* Richard Barrett, 1998

task because I know how much it will mean to the team. Teamwork is a personal value—it gives me energy and drives my performance.

The key to success for leaders is to awaken the human values in the organization and hold people accountable for using them in making decisions, their management style, and how they work with others. It takes conscious awareness to be a values-based leader. The challenge is in living your values consistently, with purity, and "walking the talk" 24/7. If you don't live the values you believe in, the way you behave will be incongruent and your organization will not have a role model to follow. It is much like parenting. If you say to your children it is important to tell the truth and they hear you lie, what message does this send to them? Leaders must be the example and role model for the values and behaviors they want the organization to espouse.

There are four pillars in society—politics, business, faith-based organizations, and civil society. To have the most desired organizational transformation, values and ethics needs to percolate in all four pillars. Values and ethics need to be inculcated, cultivated, and nurtured. It is like watering the roots of a tree for it to grow tall and strong. The seed is already present in every human being—it just needs a little nurturing. With the four institutions working together, we can make a difference this century.

Belongingness through Engagement

When I feel a positive emotional connection to another person there is a feeling of belongingness. Take for example your family. You feel they belong to you. No choice in the matter. Uncles, aunts, cousins, sisters, brothers—they all belong to you, don't they? You can't change the fact. There is a sense of kinship among these people.

I was 16 years old when I met my European cousins for the first time. The love and acceptance they made me feel was amazing. It was such a powerful feeling of connection. There was a very strong sense of family and "you are one of us." My qualities did not matter. The fact that I could not speak the language perfectly was insignificant. That I came from another country with a different education and wore different clothes did not matter. We were all family. I felt so much love and acceptance for who I was even though it was the first time meeting them. This is belongingness.

With belongingness comes the feeling of caring, trust, ownership, and wanting to take responsibility for another person, team, and organization. People will feel this sense of belongingness in different degrees depending on what the leaders and managers have done to develop and earn their trust. It's a huge benefit for the organization when people want to take responsibility and ownership for problems. Imagine your employee coming up to you with an idea that could provide substantial cost savings. Or they let you know when a major client is extremely unhappy about a late shipment, product, or service. They trust how you will respond and know there will not be any negative repercussions, such as shooting the messenger.

We all have the ability to respond in a given situation. Responsibility is our ability to respond.

Who has the most responsibility in a company? The CEO. The buck stops on their desk. This empowers them to take ownership and care for the whole organization. We all have the power to take ownership within our sphere of influence. We all have the ability to make a difference and care for others. What prevents us is not being emotionally engaged and empowered. Without the emotional trust connection, we are not likely to stick our necks out and take responsibility, to own the problem and try and find solutions.

Belongingness is created through engagement. When I show I care about you and empathize with what is important in your world, I am making an emotional, heart-centered connection with you. If you and I are having a conversation and I am actively listening to you tell a funny story, can you feel this connection? Certainly! Our eyes are connecting; my head, facial expressions and body are moving and following what you are saying. I am laughing and sharing the emotions you are sharing with me. The opposite is true as well. If my mind wanders off and leaves the room, can you feel it? Yes! It feels like you are speaking into an empty space. I may be physically in front of you, but mentally my mind is somewhere else.

Consciously engaging with someone and actively listening to them creates a sense of connection and belongingness. This creates an internal sense of cohesion between the two people that is very powerful in sustaining a healthy relationship. Having this internal cohesion is the basis for developing trust relationships, which are the foundation for high performing teams.

For a long time leaders have felt that showing or connecting with one's emotions would make them vulnerable. This is changing. Leaders are recognizing the important role of emotions in connecting and engaging people. Take the manager/employee relationship. The most important person to an employee in an organization is their manager. This is because the relationship between these two people is the deepest. It is both emotional and rational with a high degree of trust that has been developed over a long period of time. The manager is there for the employee, responsible for meeting the employee's basic needs of financial security, providing information about what is going on in the organization, ensuring they have the knowledge, expertise and resources to perform their job well, providing teamwork when needed, being responsible for commitments, and having a high degree of trust and trustworthiness.

Commitment through Alignment

With awareness and belongingness comes commitment. I'm not talking about "buy-in" to an idea, rather full commitment with the heart and mind engaged. Awareness through measurement provides the information or data needed to make critical decisions. Belongingness through engagement creates an emotional connection that builds trust and internal cohesion. Awareness and belongingness are pre-requisites to commitment. Without them it will not be possible to commit.

Suppose I come to you as my manager and share an idea for a project I am clearly quite excited about. Without a doubt I've been working on this idea for some time. I share all the details and research I've done making sure to point out the benefits to the team and organization. My tone of voice is higher than normal, I'm speaking fast, and there's a bit of a tremor as I'm a bit nervous speaking with you about it for the first time. My enthusiasm is infectious and it's even rubbing off on you. The atmosphere in the room changes subtly as you begin to actively listen to the benefits of the project. With every good point I'm making, you nod your head in agreement, and eventually you begin contributing possibilities and opportunities it will open up for everyone. I can sense your level of commitment is increasing when finally you pop the question—how much will this cost us?

Before committing to the project you go through a critical thinking process weighing the financial merits of the idea and how well it's aligned with the shared vision and mandate of your team. On the emotional level, which you may or may not have been aware of, you are assessing the idea against your personal values. How will it meet your needs as a leader and the needs of your team? Clearly I care a great deal about the project and the benefits it will bring. With years of devoted service under my belt and past project successes, you have a deep sense of trust in my ability. The key elements in gaining your commitment are alignment with mission, vision and values, accompanied by trust and internal cohesion. If the project does not meet these needs, even if it has financial merit, what is the likelihood of gaining your commitment? None.

The importance of alignment in attaining commitment is critical. With mission and vision alignment I know the actions I am taking and the work I am doing will get me to where I want to go. Mission alignment creates a shared sense of mission and purpose. It gives meaning to life and everyday tasks. I can see how my efforts will make a difference and add value to the work we are all doing. Even the most mundane tasks can seem special when they are connected to a higher goal of contributing to something bigger than oneself. I don't feel like I'm spinning wheels doing work that will not be of value to someone or will sit on a shelf collecting dust. When my values are aligned with the organization's values, there is an internal sense of connection and the feeling that everything is right with the world. I will do everything in my power to make the project happen.

As mentioned above, alignment of values, behavior, structure, processes, mission, and vision are all essential for building engagement and commitment, on both an individual and an organizational level. Suppose we have a team meeting where members agreed that decisions on a project will need to be made by building consensus. As the team leader, I now have to ensure that decisions going forward are brought to the group for discussion and reflection before decisions are made. What do you suppose would happen if I unilaterally made a decision without informing the group? Would I be "walking the talk" and living a shared value we all committed and agreed to? No. The trust that team members developed in creating the value together would be broken. What impact would this have on the team? Think of a time when your trust was broken. Did it not reduce your level of energy and cause frustration and internal conflict? This is a simple example to show how essential it is for leaders to think about the consequences and messages they are communicating in their actions.

When actions and behaviors are not in alignment with the agreed-upon values, commitment and engagement will suffer.

Commitment through alignment generates higher performance. When I am committed to an organization it will show up in various ways. As a leader I will care about the needs of my people in different areas identified in a hierarchy of values and personal motivations. The impact of this commitment will be felt across the organization. When people feel supported it makes a huge difference in their mental attitude. Positivity, enthusiasm, and energy increase. The following is a list of different levels of commitment and the types of needs that map to the seven levels of consciousness outlined in chapter 8:

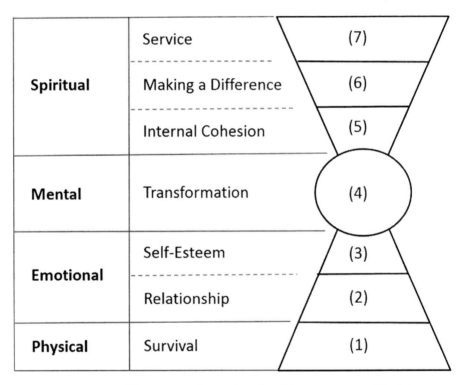

Spiritual	Service	(7)
	Making a Difference	(6)
	Internal Cohesion	(5)
Mental	Transformation	(4)
Emotional	Self-Esteem	(3)
	Relationship	(2)
Physical	Survival	(1)

Figure 1-2—The Barrett Seven Levels of Consciousness Model

1. Ensuring the health and safety of people in the organization by providing financial stability and job security for physical, mental, and emotional well-being. These are survival level of commitments that are essential to the ongoing sustainability of the organization.

2. Behaving in ways that will strengthen relationships, increase awareness and belongingness with others. Showing respect and loyalty in communications so that employees feel a sense of connectedness and family. The focus is relationship awareness to maintain effective relationships.

3. Willingness to measure employee engagement and organizational culture to find out what is happening and improve the quality, efficiency, and excellence of organizational systems and procedures. The attention is on building self-esteem of individuals.

4. Acceptance and commitment to personal and professional development recognizing adaptability and resilience to change must start at the top with senior leaders. Engaging and empowering staff by creating a culture of participation to work collaboratively, inspiring creativity and innovation. Transforming the organization with a facilitative leadership style by listening to ideas, giving people a voice in decision making, providing opportunities to grow, develop, and work as a team.

5. Communicating and owning the vision with passion and enthusiasm while living the values 24x7. The leader is consistently building trust and internal cohesion around the vision, recognizing the need to be the change they want to see.

6. Actively wanting to make a difference in the lives of people. Coaching, mentoring, and partnering, recognizing the strength and power in collaborating together to solve problems. Leaders empathize and intuitively know the needs of others, wanting to contribute in meaningful ways.

7. Concerned about global issues and actively promoting social responsibility. Having compassion for others, devoted to selfless service to society with ethical standards. Leadership is focused on being the best *for* the world not the best *in* the world.

Commitment to the above goals means living and breathing the vision, mission, and values of the organization. Leaders have to be the change they want to see. If they are not committed and in alignment with the desired values and behaviors, how can they expect others to live them. The most important level of leadership commitment is transformation at level four: supporting the transformation, emotionally connecting with staff, enabling and empowering people to continuously learn and adapt to the changes happening in the work environment. To remain competitive, leaders who are inclusive and facilitative access the wisdom of the group, engage hearts and minds, explore the implications, and decide together on the future direction with commitment and energy.

Worksheet 1-1 — Values, Beliefs and Bahaviors

Purpose: To develop self-awareness for one's personal values and the power they have to inspire greater performance.

Process: Complete a free personal values assessment (PVA) by going to: www.CultureLeadershipGroup.com/pva

Once you have received the PVA report, select your top 3 values that are the most meaningful from the list and complete the following Values and Behaviors Exercise.

Values, Beliefs and Behaviors			
Choose the top three values from your Personal Values Assessment.	What is important to you about this value?	Recall a moment in your life when you were living this value. What behaviors did you exhibit that support this value?	How might you react if this value was ignored by others? Describe your feelings.
1.)			
2.)			
3.)			

Team-Building Conversation

Objective: To demonstrate the power of values in generating new awareness, belongingness and commitment, and create a team charter that will support the team's growth and development.

Awareness: Debrief after having participants complete the Values and Behaviors exercise:
- Ask team members to pair up with another person and share their values, beliefs and behaviors with each other.
- Next form larger groups by bringing together three pairs into a group of six and ask each pair to share their values.

Belongingness: As a large group, share answers to the following questions:
1. How do you feel when you are living your personal values at work?
2. Are there any values you are not able to live? What fears do you have?
3. When you are living your values, how do they impact your performance?
4. What would happen if you were not able to bring these values to work? How would you feel? What would happen to your performance?
5. Would you want to continue working there?

Commitment: Create a team charter:
1. Group and theme the top values of team members.
2. Revisit the mission and vision of the team. How do you contribute to the organization? What are you hoping to achieve in two to three years?
3. Select three to four top values and identify three behaviors for each top value that demonstrate your values in action to support the mission and vision of your team.
4. What's one thing you can start doing tomorrow to live these values?

Chapter 2

The Cultural Divide

When we are no longer able to change a situation
— we are challenged to change ourselves.
—**Viktor E. Frankl**

Natural Tensions and Conflict

O rganizational cultures, especially in bigger organizations are made up of many sub-cultures and many different "group personalities." This is especially the case in organizations with different divisions, but also in organizations with (physically) separate departments in different countries around the world. Each division has its own mandate, set of values and behaviors that empower it to achieve goals. You may work in corporate services in Human Resources alongside Communications, Information Management, and Finance.

These services might actually reside and function in different countries with different values and expected behaviors related to that country. Each team has a specific mandate, set of objectives, or terms of reference that are aligned to the organization's overall mission, purpose, or reason for being. This cultural diversity can provide real benefits and challenges. Organizations who invest in developing their culture consciously to ensure people work effectively together across cultural diversity are more successful.[6]

I started my career as an Information Technology (IT) pre-sales consultant, working for the number two technology company in the world. It was a technical job, with a people focus. Office automation was just being introduced into the workplace, and solutions that came out of product development were my responsibility to learn and promote to clients. Sales representatives would bring me to customer meetings to provide technical details and assist in developing trust relationships. Back at the office, I would give presentations and demonstrations on the benefits of the new technology to customers in different business functions and IT groups.

It was an exciting job at times. I got to travel with clients to headquarters in Boston in company jets and take helicopter rides over rush hour traffic from the local airport to headquarter offices. Those were the days when clients would spend half a million on one server and there weren't the spending restrictions for business and government there are today. These visits would involve major IT transformations with multi-million dollar financial commitments. Hence the visit to corporate headquarters to meet with top executives, and to develop relationships with the hardware and software developers.

As a pre-sales consultant I worked between two groups with very different cultures. They were the business functions (with application requirements and budget) who needed to invest in new technology to meet their business objectives, and the IT department with the technology and expertise for implementing the solutions.

It makes perfect sense to think these two groups would be motivated to support and collaborate effectively to meet the business requirements. "You have the money; I have the toys, let's play." However, this could not have been further from the truth. To be quite honest, it felt like I was working in a war zone. Even after all these years of new information technology being introduced

6   Conscious Capitalism, John MacKay and Raj Sisodia, pg. 283

into organizations, these groups continue to have difficult relationships, often plagued with animosity, frustration, and misunderstanding.

This is a perfect example of a cultural divide and the impact when different organizational cultures collide. Why is this? There are many reasons that boil down to differences in the way people communicate and work. They have business processes that have been developed based on best practices, guiding principles, education, operating values, beliefs, and cultural norms that are not the same. The language and buzz words they use to communicate are different, along with their habits, traditions, strengths, attitudes, and emotions. These differences are the reason behaviors of each group are not understood and this lack of understanding causes a great deal of conflict. When your values are not understood, it feels like they are being ignored or stepped on, which creates conflict and deepens the challenge to work collaboratively and harmoniously.

Bottom line, groups and nationalities have distinct personalities that come out in how they think, communicate, and do things. This is how culture is defined and why cultural divides exist. Every organization suffers from some form of cultural divide unless steps are taken to invest in culture and consciously work together to develop greater awareness and appreciation for each other's differences and diversity of strengths.

One example of this kind of cultural divide happened while I was working with a client to develop an online web application for payroll service providers. The government agency was tasked with moving from a paper-based system to gather employment data to an electronic process that would generate huge savings and efficiencies. The sooner they could receive electronic data from the payroll service providers the sooner they could begin realizing these cost savings.

I advised the government client they would not be able to rush the process because data integrity is an intrinsic value for Information Management professionals. Every cell in my body knew this to be true. In every way possible I tried to educate my client to make them aware of the importance of this value. Sure enough, the payroll service providers extended the delivery schedule of the application development by six months to develop the business processes that would ensure data integrity and the collection of clean data. This caused a great deal of frustration and angst during the application development discussions between the two groups because clean data was not a requirement until phase 2 of the project. First and foremost they wanted to receive the data electronically to begin reaping the benefit and efficiencies.

Another example where cultural divides exist is in multi-national corporations. An executive team can have five to ten different nationalities all working together. A management team can have twenty different nationalities. A clash in cultures is sure to exist, very similar to the one that exists between business functions in a company with one nationality. A business process such as setting sales targets, which seems simple enough, can result in challenging conversations, misunderstanding and failed expectations depending on whether you are from Asia or the West. In Asia, a target is set based on numbers one expects to achieve. In the West, targets are set based on numbers that leaders aspire to achieve. If only 70 to 80% of the targets are achieved, the Asian mindset sees a failure to meet their numbers. In the West, this is deemed acceptable because the target was a long-range aspiration.

Problems and conflict like this arise when differences are not valued, understood, or appreciated. "Walk in a mile in my shoes" is a saying that goes a long way in business and in building relationships. An example of this is the TV show *Undercover Boss*, where CEOs take the role of frontline employees in the organization. In seeing an organization from the bottom instead of the top, leaders receive a lot of valuable feedback and information that can be gained when seeing things from other people's perspective. It takes a wise person to value diversity and accept that differences might be strengths, experience or knowledge the other person has which they do not.

All too often we keep our values buried beneath the surface. We do not make the time to examine them or see how they could be supporting us in our day-to-day exchanges. By making values explicit and managing teams based on desired organizational values, we empower everyone in the organization. Everyone will learn what respect, commitment, and trust are meant to look and feel like, and they share with you the impact when a value is broken or being lived. The process of making values explicit means having the conversation about what they mean to people and the behaviors that will show they are being respected.

Most if not all transformations entail an enormous amount of time, money, and personal commitment from the whole organization to be successful. On average, the industry rate of successful IT project implementations is around

45%. This statistic has not changed in the past forty years. Why is successful implementation of strategic initiatives so hard to achieve? Studies show cultural change as the number one reason implementations fail because leaders underestimate the investment it takes to ensure staff members take different actions or demonstrate different behaviors. This is cultural transformation.

Bridging the Cultural Divide

The most successful projects I have worked on in my career were the ones that made a large investment in managing the impact of change on their people. These included a personal commitment by the leaders to understand the challenges the employees would be going through. Along with a significant financial commitment, leaders need to invest emotionally in "engagement" communications. The purpose of engagement communications is to raise awareness, calm fears, and develop a desire for new skills and capabilities to support people emotionally during the implementation and transition.

On one of these transformation projects I got to travel across the country visiting each office as part of a travelling road show. In the morning, staff heard about the history of the project and why, what, and how the new technology was selected. In the afternoon, they received a demonstration of the new office technology system. Imagine what it must have felt like knowing your typewriter was going to be taken away and in its place you would be receiving an electronic keyboard and screen. I know this dates me; however, it meant significant change for every member of the organization.

The road show was a terrific success on many levels. It shared information, giving people the data they needed to understand why change was necessary. It showed willingness for openness and transparency in the decision-making process, as the leaders were present answering many questions. It started to build trust relationships between the business functions and IT Support groups, a necessary component for good communication and harmonious collaboration. The roadshow presented how the new systems and processes were going to function so people could begin to understand the new expectations and how their jobs were going to change.

Above all it demonstrated to staff how much their leaders cared about them and showed the leaders' willingness to understand the emotional impact this change would have.

As a leader, showing you care goes a very long way to building trust and a sense of belongingness with staff. It provides the opportunity for people to voice their concerns and hear what will be done to take care of them. It's often the heart-to-heart opportunities to communicate that have the most profound effect in building trust and a strong sense of commitment. This emotional commitment will carry you through the many challenges that are sure to happen on projects.

My career took a right turn when I got into knowledge management and met a consultant who was building a new team and looking for others interested in fulfilling the same role on projects. She was a professional facilitator providing facilitative leadership communication. When I heard her describe all the activities and added value she provided in the communication process I knew I had found my "dharma," my reason for being.

This was the answer to bridging the cultural divide. By using inclusive, participatory communication processes, group facilitation enables people to build common understanding, shared visions, and shared values. It connects people intellectually and emotionally, opening minds to new perspectives, creating synergy and opportunities for collaboration. Building trust, strengthening relationships, and generating a sense of connectedness are key ingredients to sustaining an organization and empowering them to move together cohesively towards common goals.

Culture Defined

Culture is all around us and in every organization. In order to measure, analyze, and manage culture it is important to have a definition you can apply to the organization as well as the leaders and employees. I often think of culture as the collective personality of the leadership and people within the organization. This immediately poses the question whether personality can be a collective item. To answer this question let's take a closer look at the aspects of personality I am referring to.

Personality is formed by the personal beliefs, motivational values and behaviors of an individual. These determine how the person thinks about things, does things and associates things to each other. As social groups we share personal values and behaviors. In having shared beliefs, values, and behaviors we interact with one another in ways we find acceptable that bring us closer together and create common bonds from shared experiences. When we accept the beliefs, values, and behaviors of others we recognize a piece of ourselves in other people.

Example: Trust in many cases is highly valued between friends or colleagues. There is a good reason for this value to be present between people. If I trust you, it implies that on some level you will also trust me. When trust is present in organizations this indicates a high degree of awareness, belongingness, commitment, and effective teamwork. Work is more efficient and cost-effective because there is less questioning of why decisions are being made. Costly overhead systems and processes can be reduced because we trust each other and our mutual ability to do the job. Everyone is on the same page and there is a common understanding of the way things are done.

Relationships start by exchanging information. The colleagues or partners will start by telling each other about their experiences, exchanging information about their work, the schools they attended, and associations they belong to. All of this information is essential in determining whether the person you are about to work with has a compatible set of beliefs, values, and norms of behavior. In knowing the patterns of behavior and values of your colleague or potential partner, you can anticipate how he or she will react to your own behavior and eventually adapt in order to be able to work together. In friendships or other forms of partnership, this process is almost automatic. Relationships in the personal sphere are mostly one on one, making the sharing and adapting to each other's beliefs, values and norms of behavior easier than in an organizational setup.

So far we've seen that culture encompasses sharing of beliefs, values, and behaviors. These aspects of culture are essential in the measurement, analysis, and transformation of organizational culture.

There are three dimensions that I want to focus on in this process:

1. The personal aspect: e.g. personal beliefs, values, and behavioral norms;
2. Organizational cultural aspects: current and desired values and behaviors;
3. Organization's mission / vision and strategies.

In transforming organizational culture, it is important to acknowledge that individual employees have their own sets of beliefs, motivational values, and behaviors. Motivational values determine how and why people work in certain ways, what motivates them, and gives them a sense of purpose. It is important to know what the personal values and behaviors are to know how to align them with the core values of the organization. The more alignment there is between the personal values of individuals and the organization's values, the more committed and engaged people will feel. This is because personal values are energizing and give people a sense of self-worth. The more personal values can show up in the way people work together the more engaged and high performing they will be.

People work together in organizations to attain strategic goals. Your mission, vision, and strategies will determine these goals and presume certain attitudes and behavioral norms. These presupposed or expected attitudes and behaviors are sometimes explicit and sometimes implicit. In this book I intend to show how misalignment of personal and organizational values and expected norms of behavior can be a source of frustration, disengagement, retention issues, stress, and burn out. Alignment between these three dimensions is essential in the process of reshaping the organizational culture to meet your goals.

In a ten-year study of companies conducted by Bridge's Business Consultancy[7], it was found nine out of ten strategic initiatives failed because leadership and management did not ensure staff members take different actions or demonstrate different behaviors. This implies new values were needed that would lead to different behaviors to support new strategies and goals. The toughest challenge leaders considered was changing people's values and behaviors. This is what makes cultural transformation so complex and one of the most challenging things for leaders to accomplish when implementing new strategies. Leaders need to lead the organization through an explicit process that will identify the new desired values and behaviors and why they are important to the long-term success of the organization. In this process an effort is made to align the personal

---

7   **What Drives Strategy Implementation? Top Line Findings- Bridges 10 years Implementation Survey Results, Bridges Business Consultancy Int Pte Ltd,**

values of staff to the organizational values selected to successfully implement the mission, vision, and new strategies.

When planning to transform organizational values, knowing what the leadership culture is like and how it is affecting the rest of the organization is a critical piece in this process. This is because "organizational transformation begins with the personal transformation of the leaders. Organizations don't transform, people do". [8]

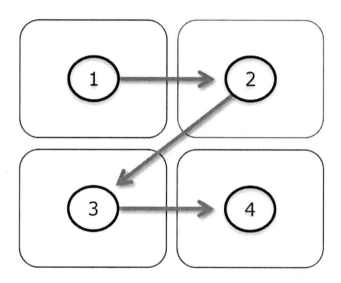

Figure 2-1—Wilber's Four Quadrants

When leaders change their beliefs and values: (1). their behaviors change; (2). the behavior change influences the culture of the group; (3). the culture change in turn changes the behaviors of the group (4).

There is a direct link between leadership style and the current organizational culture. The mission, vision, and strategies of the organization are determined and driven by the leadership team. How the strategies are implemented, the way decisions are made, and how leaders interact with staff will greatly determine the structures, processes, and policies of how people work together towards change.

---

8   The Values-Driven Organization, Richard Barrett, 2013

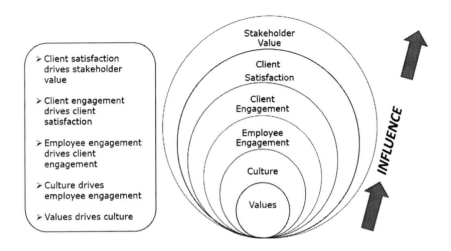

Figure 2-2—The Value Chain

In figure 2-2 we see values are at the core and have the greatest influence on creating organizational culture. Culture drives the level of employee engagement and enthusiasm. Employee engagement determines the quality of the client experience and level of customer satisfaction. Customer satisfaction determines the eventual shareholder value.

For these reasons alignment of personal values begins with the personal alignment of the leaders. They need to be able to lead themselves before they can lead others. With self-mastery and a deeper understanding of how their values are showing up in the workplace, leaders are able to see how their own level of entropy may be impacting performance. With coaching and leadership development, leaders can become the change they want to see in the whole organization. Transforming an existing culture into a desired organizational culture, begins with awareness of the current organizational values and the impact they are having. The end goal is to create a shared vision of the desired values and behaviors in action. The work for leaders and managers is to develop a common understanding of the shared values, what they will look like in action and how they will benefit the organization. This takes time and commitment to the process of facilitated dialogue, which generates new awareness, sense of belonging, and ownership of the new values.

To download free exclusive leadership development resources and valuable case studies, become a member at: www.CultureLeadershipGroup.com

Worksheet 2-1 — Impact of Diverse Cultures

Purpose: To identify and explore different impacts of diverse cultures within your organization.

Do you have different departments, functions, or nationalities within your organization? List the different departments, business functions and nationalities.
How do these departments, functions, and nationalities differ from one another? What do they value that is the same and not the same?
How have you noticed these departments, functions and nationalities colliding with one another? What impact do the different values have in creating conflict?
How would you like the relationship to be different? What's one thing you would change if you could?

Chapter 3

Beneath the Surface

The victim mindset dilutes the human potential. By not accepting personal responsibility for our circumstances, we greatly reduce our power to change them.

— **Steve Maraboli**

Corporate Life Force

Corporate life force is a powerful current beneath the surface in organizations. It is the energy in organizational values that enlivens the human spirit with positivity, gives guidance and direction in times of difficulty, and creates a sense of connection. Like a mighty river, the current beneath the surface is a force of nature. As a client looking from the river bank, you are aware of the force, you can sense it and the strength of what is happening beneath the surface, but you cannot see it.

When you are in it, this force is very real. If there are limiting values such as control, greed, manipulation, hierarchy, and bureaucracy, these values and behaviors will have the effect of sucking the life force energy out of people daily. This makes it difficult to excel, be creative and give 100%.

On the other end of the spectrum, when the work environment is living the values of respect, transparency, collaboration, commitment, ownership, trust, shared vision, leadership, employee fulfillment, and making a difference, the positive energy in this kind of atmosphere fuels performance. People come to work loving their job. To create this kind of environment takes leadership with full spectrum values.

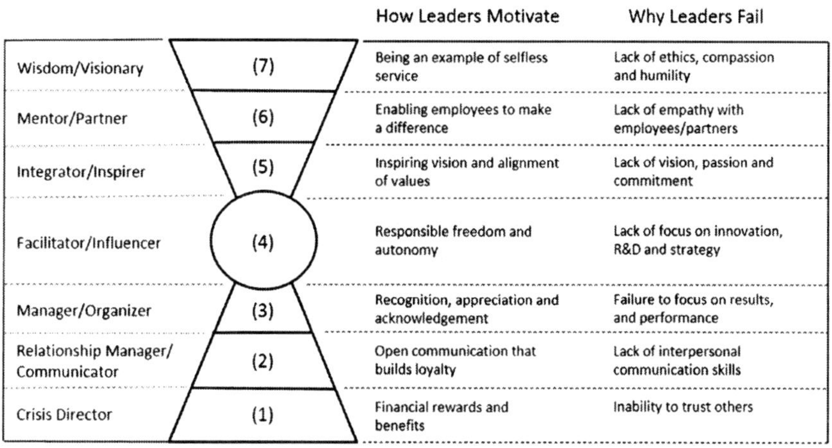

		How Leaders Motivate	Why Leaders Fail
Wisdom/Visionary	(7)	Being an example of selfless service	Lack of ethics, compassion and humility
Mentor/Partner	(6)	Enabling employees to make a difference	Lack of empathy with employees/partners
Integrator/Inspirer	(5)	Inspiring vision and alignment of values	Lack of vision, passion and commitment
Facilitator/Influencer	(4)	Responsible freedom and autonomy	Lack of focus on innovation, R&D and strategy
Manager/Organizer	(3)	Recognition, appreciation and acknowledgement	Failure to focus on results, and performance
Relationship Manager/ Communicator	(2)	Open communication that builds loyalty	Lack of interpersonal communication skills
Crisis Director	(1)	Financial rewards and benefits	Inability to trust others

Figure 3-1—The Barrett Seven Levels of Leadership Model

A leader must walk the talk and be a role model for the values and behaviors they want for the organization. It takes flawless devotion to living the values to successfully transform a culture. Cynicism will quickly set in if employees see anything else. On the journey to transform your culture it is imperative that leaders develop awareness of their own personal values, to be in tune with what they are missing and to create greater personal alignment with the desired new organizational values. New values need to be developed in the leaders first and then rolled out to the management team. For this reason, coaching, mentoring, and personal development are necessary tools for leadership to be able to lead themselves effectively before they can lead others. Chapter 8 describes the Leadership Values Assessment that is available for coaching and mentoring.

A corporate example of this life force and leadership can be found in Lenovo Corporation. In 2012 and 2013, the CEO shared $3 million from his personal annual bonus with 10,000 of his employees. The two organizational values in Lenovo that provide corporate life force to support this behavior are commitment and ownership. A brief history of Lenovo—when Lenovo purchased the IBM ThinkPad in 2005, two corporate cultures, East and West, (China and USA) were merged. At the time, there was significant skepticism in the business community about the long-term sustainability of the merger due to the vast difference between these two cultures.

Many mergers and acquisitions fail to realize the anticipated value of a merger because joining two cultures to create something new is challenging. Research suggests that between 60 to 80% of mergers fail to live up to initial expectations. There are several key reasons for this and one of the biggest reasons is the failure of the leadership of the new company to integrate the two distinct cultures to create one organization. It takes a committed leadership team and significant financial investment in cultural transformation for mergers to succeed.

Eight years after the Lenovo/IBM merger, Lenovo is the number one PC vendor in China and growing in global markets. There have been and continue to be values programs and management training to build trust and understanding between the different cultures. Every effort is made to shift mindsets and make people sensitive to the needs of the others in the work environment.

For example, there is a twelve-hour time zone difference between China and the United States. Teams in each location take turns on the late night conference calls. The business language is English. People from the West are mindful to speak slowly and enunciate their words for their colleagues to whom English is a second language.

Corporate life force is about living your values in service of others. As a facilitative leader my mindset and values are focused on the people in the group I am serving. Another term often used for facilitative leadership is servant leadership. This is demonstrated in the mindset of facilitators. For example, self-respect is good; however, respect for others is more powerful. Being honest is good; however, honesty and transparency to others is more powerful. Being responsible for oneself is good; however, being responsible for others is more powerful.

Commitment and ownership are values on which Lenovo was founded. When you feel a sense of ownership towards something you tend to take more responsibility for it. The current CEO has been investing in company stocks since he joined the firm in 1989; he now owns 8% of the company. In giving $3 million of his personal bonus to 10,000 employees as a form of employee recognition, the CEO was infusing more fuel into the corporate life force of these values. The reward had significant impact on strengthening employee engagement and the company's reputation and brand. Providing employee recognition rewards and ensuring employees are fulfilled, are leadership competencies that make a difference and boost morale, mental attitude, and performance. Employees are very proud of their company and CEO.

Demonstrating the values of commitment and ownership in this visible and tangible way to external stakeholders differentiates the company from its competitors. It builds confidence in investors, suppliers, and customers, all of which goes a long way to strengthening the brand in a very competitive marketplace. Lenovo is a role model for sharing the wealth and recognizing those on whom you rely to be successful. Internally it reinforces the organizational values of commitment and ownership. Externally it reinforces the brand.

Obstacles to creating and engineering corporate life force are fears, doubt, traditions, and control, to name just a few behaviors. Old styles of management and leadership are being replaced by facilitative servant leadership designed to engage and empower employees.

In today's knowledge economy with the power of the internet and matrix, networked organizations, it is not possible to know it all. To remain competitive, people must work effectively in teams with team leaders who are skilled in facilitation methods. To build the most effective teams, team leaders must build trust relationships, and use methods that access the wisdom of the group. They must demonstrate the values of respectful communications, active listening, open mindedness, and have the ability to ask open-ended questions that probe beneath the surface and create high impact results.

Facilitative leadership means letting go of control, trusting that the group will come up with the right answers, and when they do, the group will have more commitment to and ownership of the solutions. This leads to increased collective action and high performance in carrying out decisions.

In working together as a team the corporate life force is stronger. The strengths and values of each team member are combined and connected, resulting in more creativity to put towards problem solving and stronger commitment in decision making. This takes conscious awareness and respect for the strengths and values of one's self and attention to the strengths and values of others on the team.

Teams are usually made up of members with different personalities and motivational values. Diversity is a strength that will benefit the team in the long run as different strengths can be called upon at different times. However, diversity is often a challenge for leaders to manage and a challenge for group members to appreciate and respect the different perspectives of others.

For example, as a leader I may be motivated by results and don't mind taking a few risks when going after new opportunities. Others in the group may be risk averse and need time to research before committing to plans, while some others may have a focus on the impact the decision will have on people and relationships. It is important to be respectful and attentive to the personal motivating values of others and seek ways to facilitate alignment of personal values in the meeting process and decision making.

Values, Beliefs, and Behaviors in Action

The life force in values connects to a person's spirit, being or essence. Values connect people together and they connect the human spirit. Like the mighty force of a river in nature, we have a power within us that is beyond measure. We call upon it in times of extreme need and it empowers us with tremendous strength. We've all heard the stories of a mother who lifted a car to retrieve her baby from harm's way, or the bravery of a fireman who defies death and safely brings survivors out of a burning building.

When we focus our values on others we get stronger and more powerful, as the examples above highlight. When I trust myself this is good; however, when I trust others this is more powerful. When I am able to lead myself, this is good; however, to be able to lead others is more powerful.

To build a high performing culture, leaders need to shift the focus from "me" (self-interest) to "we" (common good for all)—a shift from being the best *in* the world to being the best *for* the world. When we live our values in service of others, we are making this world a better place in which to live. The human spirit is a powerful force. When focused on the collective power in "we," it can achieve anything it wants to. When focused on "me" it creates separation, distance, disharmony, and competition in a group. This can lead to a toxic work environment filled with stress, frustration, depression, and anxiety.

The problems in society today stem from too much focus on "me" (self-interest) and on competition—being the best in the world; the "me" culture, is contributing to a toxic work environment as people continually seek more success and gratification for themselves. We see the effects of this in society by the increase in addiction to drugs and alcohol, divorce, poverty, violence, burnout, and disease. Being the best in the world is a never-ending cycle of trying to meet illusive goals and needs that never feel truly fulfilled.

An attitude of being the best for the world lifts people's spirits and has a completely different effect. When I do something for someone else I immediately feel joy at seeing the impact of helping others. The appreciation and human contact is heartfelt. The spirit expands and feels empowered by having made a positive contribution to another person's life, no matter the action. It could be opening a door or saying "thank you" with a smile. People appreciate the kindness and thoughtfulness.

The more awareness, concern, and consciousness leaders develop in their own personal values and the personal values of their people, the more they will become aware of the power in values. Inside organizations, leaders have consciously been living disconnected from their personal values. This is because personal values have been seen as soft and not in alignment with the behaviors required in being competitive.

Values define a person and what is important to them. When you live in alignment with your values, life has a sense of purpose and is meaningful. The same is true for living the organizational values. Living the values creates value.

For example, when an organization lives the values of honesty and transparency, this can be defined by full disclosure of facts and operations. In living these values in synch with the organization, employees build trust in their leaders and share information that leads to greater efficiency in production processes, reducing overhead costs, shortening customer delivery schedules, increasing customer satisfaction and shareholder value. On the downside, if these values are not valued and are instead ignored, these desired behaviors are less likely to be in evidence.

New thinking patterns and degrees of intelligence emerge as consciousness is developed and expanded. With greater capacity and discernment, the importance and care towards others grows. Stronger interpersonal relationships foster more harmonious teamwork. Increased level of intelligence and consciousness make it possible to develop new strategies to solve problems.

Difference in Mindset and Attitudes Between "Me" and "We"[9]

Me	We
Accumulation	Growth
Acquires	Savors
Remembers	Reflects
Maintains	Evolves
Thinks	Processes
Blames	Takes responsibility
Ruled by emotions/wants	Ruled by reason/inspiration
Recalls events	Contextualizes significance
Plans	Creates
Definition	Essence, meaning
Motivation	Inspiration, intention
Morals	Ethics
Physical & emotional survival	Intellectual development
Pleasure and satisfaction	Fulfillment of potential
Impatience	Tolerance
Demands	Prefers
Controls	Surrenders
Literal	Intuitive
Competition	Cooperation
Excess	Balance
Force	Power
Exploits life	Serves life
Callous	Merciful
Insensitive	Sensitive
Closed	Open-ended

9   Transcending the Levels of Consciousness, David Hawkins, M.D. Ph.D. 2006

Wants	Chooses
Sympathizes	Empathizes
Avoids	Faces and accepts
Critical	Accepting
Attacks	Avoids
Condemning	Forgiving
Guarded	Friendly
Cynical	Optimistic
Selfish	Considerate

Our values and attitudes (mindset) have an impact on how we see the world. We all have limiting values and attitudes, and positive values and attitudes. The power in doing an organizational or leadership values assessment is the support it generates for developing what we want more of in our culture. The effects of limiting values begin to diminish as soon as they are recognized and owned.

The benefit of accepting one's limiting values is an inner sense of self-acceptance, honesty, and higher self-esteem. When I know my limitations, I am less sensitive to negative opinions others may have about me. A self-honest person is less prone to having their feelings hurt or having a "bone to pick" with others. When people admit their weaknesses, others cannot attack them. As a result, one feels less vulnerable, safer, and more secure. This is true for organizations as a whole and for leaders.

Positive Personal Traits to Develop[10]

Available	Equitable	Balanced	Ethical
Fair	Calm	Faithful	Considerate
Firm	Content	Flexible	Cordial
Friendly	Decent	Genuine	Dependable
Glad	Happy	Diplomatic	Easygoing
Helpful	Honest	Reliable	Humane
Respectable	Responsible	Kind	Sense of humor
Open	Sensible	Compassionate	Supportive
Pleasing	Pleasant	Polite	Positive

10   Transcending the Levels of Consciousness, David Hawkins, M.D. Ph.D. 2006

| Persistent | Stable | Wisdom |

It takes courage for leaders to start a journey of cultural transformation. It is challenging, exciting, and stimulating all at the same time. Courage implies the willingness to try new things and deal with the challenges that will be uncovered in the process of discovery. Having courage brings with it the energy to learn new things and try out new behaviors. It also gives people the confidence to face their fears.

When people have courage they are giving back to the organization as much as they are taking. In having the courage to try new things, they achieve more. In achieving more results they increase their self-esteem and receive positive feedback from their peers. This has the effect of increasing the life force energy and this is where high performance and productivity begins.

Values Table

The following comments from individuals give some contextual data on the power of values to engage, motivate and retain employees.

Table 3-1 — Power of Values

Why is this value important to you?	What behaviors do you exhibit that support this value?	How does it feel when you are able to live this *value*?	If this value was ignored or disrespected by your organization, how would you feel and would you want to continue working there?
Value – *Respect*			
Without respect all our efforts are meaningless.	Respect is the very foundation of my actions.	I feel worthy of people and being respected in return.	Shocked! No.

Value – *Family*			
Continuity is the most important thing in life. I do everything for my family.	I take time and appreciate the moments with them to maximize the exchanges.	My family motivates me to push for more, never give up and be better for them.	I would leave if family time was not respected and valued.
Value – *Honesty*			
It is the basis for everything. If there is no honesty in what is being done and why, then it is simply a waste of precious time and energy.	Having commitment, working with passion, and sometimes may include swallowing bitter pills.	Especially when it is hard to be honest, and you are still honest with yourself and others, it is a very liberating experience. Most important to be honest with myself first.	Disappointment, lack of trust, and willingness to work with others. Suspicion and creating a distance from them. No, I would not want to continue working there.
Value – *Accountability*			
I believe people have to take responsibility for their actions both positive and negative. It is part of growing. You have to own your role in each situation, decision, and action.	Owning up to your mistakes and learning from them, taking credit for your successes, working to find solutions for issues or situations that arise	When you live this value you are proud and confident. Your self-esteem is solid.	No. When there is little or no accountability for actions in the workplace, the environment becomes a toxic place to work.

Value – *Commitment*			
In order for a workplace to soar, people need to be committed to the mission, vision, and values. Without commitment, people tend to look at their jobs as just a way to make money.	Showing up to work on time and working to get the job done instead of being a clock watcher. Truly exhibiting interest in the organization's well-being, goals, and demonstrating that through hard work and dedication.	Work is a much more peaceful and happy place when you are committed to the organization. This can translate into having a vested interest in moving the organization forward.	No. If there is little commitment, you end up with individuals who are self-serving and just looking for a paycheck.
Value – *Integrity*			
Very important to lead by example and put forth high morals and professional standards. This increases the probability that staff will follow suit. This value is important to me because it sets the tone for actions in the workplace.	Showing up on time, answering questions in a timely fashion, being honest and forthcoming, accountable for your actions, working hard, being a positive force, being transparent, looking for solutions when issues arise instead of complaining.	Proud and confident.	No. I could not work or be involved with an organization that did not have integrity because it would be impossible to be committed to the mission, vision and values if integrity was not at the forefront.

Value – *Efficiency*			
It is the manifestation of knowledge, skills, attitudes & behaviors – IN ACTION to optimize the resources of people and time.	Do a 360 degree review of issues. Optimize the resources to deliver on commitments.	Feel satisfied and it enhances my personal leadership mastery.	Feel unwanted and as if I don't belong to that place.
Value – *Responsibility*			
It is what motivates me and makes me work hard to get the goals that I set for myself. I am responsible for my life, my work, and achieving my goals	Commitment— showing up on time and showing up! Doing what you say you are going to do and not slacking. Leaders are ones who take responsibility.	I feel empowered and feel that I can take on a bigger responsibility and bigger challenges… it gives me confidence.	I tend to be short and sharp and honest with people who are "placeholders." They say they will do something but then don't. Also I then have a lack of trust in them. I would leave.
Value – *Making a Difference*			
Important to leave the world (or my part of it) a better place; to help evolve situations, and make a positive contribution.	I show up in life trying to remember that my purpose is to make things better and bring that positive view to all situations and interactions.	Feels exhilarating and alive and full of life energy.	I feel drained and sense that potential is being wasted. Wouldn't want to be there.

Value – *Compassion*			
Compassion brings out the human in me. I feel the connectedness.	Empathizing with people situations, extending the helping hand no matter how the person is.	Connected.	It really doesn't matter but I do feel taken aback. No.
Value – *Ethics*			
It personifies an intersection of values, transparency, care and respect for the entire environment.	Demonstrate the organizational citizenship for people, resources, environment and the policies.	Feel like a leader and a sense of fulfillment	Mediocrity and a sense of wasted time and resources. A sense of I don't belong to the place. No.
Value – *Wisdom*			
A lot of times I want to do something, but when I apply some wisdom to the situation, I find better ways of achieving the same goals or even better the goal.	Being open to listening, and meditating to sharpen my intuition. Reading biographies and learning from mistakes.	I feel empowered and wise! Also the experiences are amazing when actions hold wisdom in them rather than just an action to a means to an end.	I do my best to handle it with compassion as well as skill. When actions or words are said or done in ignorance, it is easy to feel compassion and correct them appropriately.

Consequences When Values Are Ignored

In all the seminars and one-on-one interviews I have given on the power of values, every person asked has said they experience an increase in positive energy when they are able to live their values. When asked if they would wish to continue working for an organization that disrespected or disregarded their values, all the respondents answered a solid NO.

Performance and culture are directly linked with engagement and retention through our values. In values-driven organizations people excel. In organizations with high entropy and limiting values such as control, manipulation, blame, hierarchy, and bureaucracy, energy is drained by the frustration and limitations the limiting values impose.

As seen in the Values Table, values are a source of inspiration and motivation. People feel alive, confident, committed, connected, empowered, energized, exhilarated, liberated, and proud. The workplace is more peaceful, happy, and productive.

Leaders often view inclusive group processes as time-consuming exercises where everyone gets together for a group hug and the opportunity to share emotions and feelings. In reality, the inclusive process provides team leaders the opportunity to explore experience, access knowledge, and build consensus and commitment. The ROI of investing time at the front end of a project gives team members the opportunity to build trust and relationships that will support the project when it runs into challenges down the road.

When the values of teambuilding, building consensus, and commitment are not valued, and they are replaced by speed and efficiency to get the job done quickly and efficiently. Individuals who are empowered by teamwork or who need to plan and do research before committing to action, will disengage and feel rejected because their values have been ignored.

Our values and motives drive our behavior. When motivational values are ignored or stepped on, this creates an internal experience of conflict. Conflict is a reaction to a perceived threat to our self-worth. The results of the Strength Deployment Inventory (SDI©). (reference Annex – Relationship Awareness Training) show how we experience motivational changes in conflict, which drive changes in behavior.

This is why sometimes you will perceive a "Dr. Jekyll and Mr. Hyde" change in people's behavior. The added challenge to conflict is our motivation can lead to behavior that escalates the conflict. The SDI© helps people understand that changes to motivation and behavior in conflict are normal, and learn how to manage conflict more effectively.

An example: When in conflict, one person may need 24 hours to analyze a problem or situation, while another person will have a strong desire to resolve the problem immediately. This difference in approach can create more conflict. But these two people can learn to more quickly recognize what is causing the problem, and come up with a reasonable timeframe and method to resolve it.

Stages of Conflict

Conflict Stage	Focus On	Nurturing	Assertive	Analytical
Stage 1	Self, Other, Problem	Accommodate the needs of others	Rise to the challenge	Be prudently cautious
Stage 2	Self, ~~Other~~, Problem	Surrender conditionally	Fight to win	Pull back to analyze
Stage 3	Self, ~~Other~~, ~~Problem~~	Feel completely defeated	Fight for survival	Retreat completely

Table 3-2 – **Internal Experience of Conflict** Reference: Strength Deployment Inventory® (SDI®), © **Personal Strengths Publishing, used with permission.**

In the book, *Have a Nice Conflict*, authors Tim Scudder, Michael Patterson, and Kent Mitchell describe the **SDI®** conflict sequence:

People are willing to go into conflict about things that are important to them. When we see conflict in other people, we can discover what is important to them.

What happens in conflict when we feel our self-worth or values are being threatened? Our motivation can change completely; we experience a sequential change in our motivation, which drives changes in our behavior, as we enter into our conflict sequence. Conflict is a sequence of predictable patterns of three progressively serious stages of change in motivation and behaviors.

Stage 1: Your attention is focused on yourself, the other person and the problem.

Stage 2: The focus narrows to yourself and the problem. *This is a very serious stage for relationships because when you no longer care about the other person with whom you are in conflict, you can do and say things that will destroy trust and the relationship. Once trust is broken it is very difficult to rebuild.*

Stage 3: The focus is only on the self. This is the most damaging stage because the individual has lost sight of the problem and the other person. Many people have only experienced Stage 3 conflict a few times in their lives. It is not a very pleasant place to be.

Conflict cannot be eliminated in our life but we can reduce conflict by being aware of the things that are important to others. We can anticipate and manage conflict that is inevitable. Ask yourself how people with different motivational values might view a situation. When two or more people view things differently there is a potential for conflict. Consider the triggers that might threaten their self-worth and push them into conflict. Preventing conflict is about deliberately interacting with people in a more productive way.

When conflict does arise, try and find out what the motivations are. Where are people coming from? What are they after? It's important to find out why someone is behaving a certain way. The goal is to find out their intent. Avoid letting misinterpretations cause more conflict. Respect where the other person is coming from.

While we are trying to find out the "right" thing to maintain our values and sense of self-worth, conflict can happen when our "right" thing is the "wrong" thing to the other person. We end up working against each other because of different motivational values, differences in style or perspective.

There is a dynamic that takes place in conflict called the Drama Triangle. We see leaders as "villains," causing us pain by disrespecting our values and imposing their will on us. Or we may feel like the "hero" and try to come up with solutions to fix the problem.

When values are ignored it creates a drama triangle that can have limiting effects on people's performance. To avoid the drama triangle, the leader can anticipate the challenge and seek to understand the situation and identify the problems before or after they occur. By knowing the values of your people, you can plan engaging communications that address the reasons you are making a decision in a particular way.

Give compelling reasons that provide information and address the emotional fears. Along with compelling reasons, provide the opportunity to discuss the decision, letting people share their experiences. Seek input—when people are given an opportunity to voice their concerns they are less likely to go into deep conflict. Some people just need time to analyze a situation and assess the risks. Not giving these types of personalities the time to analyze a situation will create conflict for them. Ask what they need and do your best to respect the needs.

Another source of conflict is when we think our values or needs are being threatened and we feel "victimized." As a victim we experience a sense of powerlessness and innocence; "this is not my fault." We might withdraw, with the flight part of "fight or flight" response, or we might wait for the "hero" to rescue us.

Some people suffer in silence, while others are more verbal and blame or complain about the situation, with a strong desire to resolve the conflict quickly. Heroes may start out wanting to protect the group and seek peace and harmony by coming up with solutions that care for the group or even the score. They have a sense of nobility and see themselves as helping others by resolving the problem. However, this attitude can turn to self-righteousness, justifying aggressive and hurtful behavior.

The third part of the drama triangle is the "villain." Villains are seen to be controlling, manipulative and deprive the victim of their values and needs. This is how the leader or manager is viewed. They are seen as selfish and controlling, out to take what they want without concern for the impact on others.

Blame, judgment, and self-righteousness are all limiting behaviors that create a toxic work environment. Stress, frustration, anxiety, and depression result. These behaviors create a win/lose attitude between people, where individuals want to compete and fight each other in a battle to win.

With a facilitative mindset and leadership skills, the leader can seek to resolve the conflict when it arises. In facilitated group discussions people are invited to voice their concerns, become aware of their fears, and take self-responsibility and ownership for how they are feeling. Providing the opportunity to voice concerns in a group gives people a chance to voice their needs instead of complaining. It is empowering to identify what we need to change the situation

Figure 3-2—The Drama Triangle

and become an active participant in the corrective actions. By voicing our needs we are becoming clearer about what our values mean to us and more aware of our actions and behaviors on others.

With the hero mindset comes the attitude of being right, "let's fix the problem my way." To resolve this mindset, people need to let go of the need to be right. Leaders can focus the attention of the group on ways to get the needs and values met. This provides opportunities for creative brainstorming and sharing past experience and knowledge to develop solutions. Problem-solving solutions created in a group, as a team, generate positive energy. The focus is on the problem and not on the people.

It takes courage to raise issues. It takes acceptance to listen to others' needs and to empathize and understand the challenges. It takes an open mind and curiosity to let go of judgment and see things from other's perspective. All these are values and behaviors a facilitative leader needs to model to resolve the consequences when values cannot be met or are perceived as being disrespected and ignored.

When working to resolve the problems together in a group setting, the focus shifts from "me" to "we," developing solutions that are good for all. In this space of common empathy and concern for all, being conscious of the corporate life force unites hearts and minds, and produces sustainable results with greater awareness, belongingness, and commitment.

To learn how you can transform conflict and
receive powerful team leadership tools, become a member at:
www.CultureLeadershipGroup.com

Worksheet 3-1 — Conflict Triggers and Resolution

Purpose: To develop self-awareness for the reasons people go into conflict and how conflict can be resolved.

What triggers conflict for you?
In Stage 1 of conflict, when you care about the problem, the other person, and yourself, what do you do?
How do you feel?
What do you really want?
What are the do's and don'ts of approaching you?

What are the costs and consequences of ignoring values?
How can conflict have a positive impact?

Part 2

Currents in the Sea of Change

Part 2 describes the current world challenges and situations that are affecting people and culture inside of organizations.

The significant problems we face cannot be solved at the same level of thinking that created them.

Figure Part 2 – New Operating Reality

Chapter 4

Core Challenges

People with high levels of personal mastery cannot afford to choose between reason and intuition or head and heart, any more than they would choose to walk on one leg or see with one eye.

—Peter Senge

How to Attract, Engage, and Retain Top Talent

Top talent is hard to find, engage, and keep. Imagine you are an MBA student looking for a new career you will love. Leaving behind a job in a company that was not fulfilling, you enrolled in the best MBA program in the country, and now you are searching for that dream position—a role that is going to inspire you with its mission and purpose, and provide the intellectual challenges that will allow you to continue to grow, develop, and contribute to society in a meaningful way.

The core challenge for organizations looking to attract top talent is fulfilling the "dream" and providing a match in leadership style and values. The traditional view of leadership has changed from previous generations. Some 80% of MBA students surveyed[11] believe their generation views leadership differently. What do you think? If you were graduating today from an MBA program, what kind of organizational culture would you be attracted to?

The first technology firm I worked for was founded by an engineer. The values of the leader permeated the whole organization. There was a deep sense of caring about quality in the products, services, and customer experience. This spilled over into how employees and customers were treated. Attention paid to our professional development paid off in our level of engagement and how we treated our clients, which in turn increased client satisfaction and shareholder value.

The values of emerging leaders are substantially different from those leaders who graduated thirty years ago. Their passions are more global with a social mindset. Young leaders see potential in globalization and partnering to drive convergence in public, private, and non-profit sectors to find solutions to the world's toughest problems. Their priority is sustainability and they believe in the power of mobile as a critical technology.

How will our young leaders shape the business of tomorrow? Full engagement and collaboration are primary values that will drive their priorities and how they prepare to meet the challenges of the future. They want to be involved in shaping the future vision of the company—one that will be inspiring, make a difference, and have a social impact.

With a focus on engagement and collaboration, emerging leaders place value on learning from listening to different perspectives they may not always agree with. They believe workplace diversity can lead to better business outcomes, especially diversity in gender, professional experience, and functional experience.

If you were to assess your culture how well would you be able to fulfill these desired values?

---

11   Passion and Purpose: Stories from the Best and Brightest Young Business Leaders by John
     Coleman, Daniel Gulati, and W. Oliver Segovia, and their survey of 500 Students from top
     U.S. business schools

The best companies today are looking for a match in values in their recruitment and on-boarding process. The more clearly defined your values and behaviors are and the more investment you make in your organization's workplace culture, the more likely you are to attract the right talent to suit your needs. The degree to which a candidate's personal values and your organizational values align will have a significant impact on the future level of engagement, performance, and job satisfaction.

Employee engagement is major concern for many organizations. It affects client engagement, client satisfaction, and shareholder value. How loyal are your clients? How much do they *love* your company's products and services? The level of employee engagement determines the quality of interaction between your clients and employees. If your people have a positive attitude and are committed to your company's products and services, this enthusiasm will be communicated in the service they provide and in client engagement.

Leaders' and managers' values and behaviors play a key role in the employee experience. Defensive leaders who blame others create an atmosphere of distrust. Those who control and manipulate the input of staff, end up frustrating the creativity and desire of employees with knowledge and experience to share.

Conversely, open and frank leaders (leaders who are inclusive, good listeners, and have a positive attitude) are able to earn high levels of engagement, trust, and commitment of employees.

The overall performance of the organization depends on the level of employee engagement, which is dependent on how stimulating the work environment is:

- Are employees supported and inspired to participate?
- Do they have goals that are stretching their talents while working on projects they feel will have impact on the organization and its mission?
- How are employee strengths and motivational values recognized by managers?
- How empowered or autonomous do employees feel in the work they do?

Creating a culture of participation and social interaction boosts employee engagement. Discussion and reflection are a form of continuous learning that is very effective at increasing awareness, belongingness, and commitment. Facilitative leadership supports transformational learning. The learning is two-way with leaders gaining access to the experience and knowledge of the group and staff learning from their peers. With increased knowledge of the problem from listening to different perspectives, employees are encouraged to take ownership and self-responsibility for new values and behaviors that lead to solutions.

Leaders who adopt a facilitative approach engage others in developing vision, building the kind of commitment that vision needs. Such leaders increase the possibility of building powerful teams that bring visions and plans into reality.

I invite you to regularly make the time to reflect and connect with your teams by having a Focused Conversation[12]. Find out what is happening with them in their lives and at work. How are they feeling about things? What are they learning that is adding value to their work? What is one thing they'd like to do differently to make work more satisfying?

Focused conversations engage people on a deep level. These conversations surface wisdom from the subconscious and increase self-awareness that makes us more consciously competent. An effective form of adult learning happens in conversation with others. Focused conversations like the one above provide diverse perspectives to problems at work and in life that everyone can connect with. Our view of the world expands and we experience a sense of sweet success in the joy of new-found knowledge and awareness.

Attracting, engaging, and retaining top talent is dependent on the ability of the organization to fulfill the promise of its commitment to employees by living organizational values. When organizational values are in place but *not* increasing employee engagement, the following could be taking place:

- One rule for senior managers and another one for everyone else
- Profit is placed ahead of organizational values
- There is no recognition of behaving in line with organizational values
- People are not disciplined or dismissed for failing to adhere to organizational values
- Values are not meaningful for employees or connected to performance results
- People do not understand the values or how they apply to them

---

12   For Group Facilitation Methods Training - www.JoannaBarclay.com/leadershipskills

It takes four-way alignment to ensure sustainable change:

1. Leadership values and behaviors are in alignment with organizational values.
2. Leaders 'walk the talk' to build trust and credibility.
3. Systems, processes and management training support are in alignment with the organizational values—for example: changing from a directive-style leadership where the leader made the decisions to a collaborative, consensus-based style of leadership would require management training in group facilitation methods to support effective group decision making and problem solving.
4. Finally, the mission and vision need to be in alignment with the organizational values, systems, and processes to ensure the change in behaviors—people doing things a different way to support new strategies.

Without this four-way alignment, transformation efforts will be superficial and will end up frustrating people who make a personal effort to change yet see the organization continuing with its old ways.

How are your people rewarded for behaving in line with organizational values? When leaders manage organizational values the same as they do financial budgets, corporate culture takes on a whole new meaning for staff. Culture becomes a corporate asset that is linked to performance.

Case in point, with ownership and commitment in place, staff have the green light to voice concerns over product manufacturing, to reduce costs or client services to improve client satisfaction. Engaging and empowering staff to live and provide feedback on the organization's ability to live its organizational values can become a source of value creation and business intelligence. This takes leadership, management attention, a watchful eye on consistency, and nurturing to develop.

Retention of employees is directly related to consistent behavior and alignment with personal values. When behavior is in line with espoused organizational values employees know what is expected of them and they can excel. When employees are not able to live their personal values and these are disrespected or ignored, this drives a spike into the heart of engagement and level of commitment, creating conflict and changes in behavior. It leads to disengagement, dissatisfaction, and reduced levels of commitment and performance.

Employee turnover due to low retention is a costly challenge for management: it entails retraining, losing employees with corporate knowledge and valuable client relationships, and damages team cohesion. Investing in values assessments and engaging staff in focused conversations to connect behaviors to values and strategic goals, lets leaders know what is important to staff. Debriefing the results provides opportunities for leaders to communicate and build deeper connections and trust with staff. When staff sense leaders honestly care about what is important to them, this strengthens their commitment and desire to reciprocate in equal measure.

Imagine one of your values is honesty. A new team leader stretches the truth to ensure the team's results look good to senior management and clients. What would it feel like not being able to experience the value of working in an honest environment? Would you want to continue working for that person? What impact would it have on your engagement and level of performance? The same can be said for companies who share financial results with investors. How much pride and enthusiasm will staff have in sharing the results when they know the real value of the company?

Creativity, Innovation, and Client Satisfaction

Increasing creativity, innovation, and client satisfaction in the face of constant change is a business necessity in the global economy and a challenge for most organizations. Every organization has to learn how to adapt quickly to developments in its surrounding environment. This in turn creates the need to become more adaptable and resilient to change. However, constant change, creativity, and innovation can be disruptive, difficult to manage, and a source of stress. It is hard to be creative when you are stressed, due to the impact of change that is causing you to disengage.

An organization going through change is usually affecting the way its people work, which can mean retraining or finding a new position inside or outside of the company. People in such situations often feel a sense of loss, fear, anxiety, insecurity, or depression.

All of these emotions affect their mental state, which has a direct impact on productivity and performance. The business challenge is: how do you keep your people engaged in the process, connected mentally and emotionally to your objectives, so they can continue being creative and innovative, doing their best to solve problems and deliver excellent client service?

Case Study – Innovation at Shell Corporation
A few years ago, Shell CEO Peter Voser laid out a bold vision for Shell to become the most innovative energy company. Inspired by this call to action, chemical engineer Mandar Apte, part of Shell's *Game Changer* program, designed the Empower initiative—an educational, staff-led curriculum that uses meditation exercises sourced from the International Association for Human Values to build individual capacity and enable creativity and innovation.

Apte: "Innovation starts with an idea, a hunch, a gut feeling. You don't really know whether it's going to be successful or if it's going to fail unless you try it. You keep doing small things one at a time and you have small wins. Even failures tell you something, so you go back and you analyze. Innovation is a process."

And with Empower, staff are provided with tools to develop greater emotional intelligence and inner resilience to improve focus and overcome failure.

Apte: "One has to learn how to drop the old habits, the old ideas, the old concepts, and taking a pause from the business of today, create a gap in your mind from the train of thoughts. That's what meditation allows you. It gives you tools and techniques to pause. The second step involves social processes and interpersonal skills. If you can invoke compassion or empathy in yourself, where you are not judging yourself, you're not criticizing yourself, nor are you judging somebody else, then I think there is a space for insights to be created. These qualities are crucial for grooming your own innovative skills and nourishing the innovation culture in an organization."

The challenge for leaders is how to measure the return on investment, and gauge the impact and success of programs like Empower. At Shell they decided to capture anecdotal evidence through stories of empowerment that changed the culture and people's work habits.

Apte: "Some stories are about how people have been able to make unique connections. By nature they may not have chosen to interact with somebody else, but through the *Empower* techniques, they have built connections that are beyond their traditional skill pool. It's through such connections that you can start thinking about non-traditional ideas. That is how you can leverage someone else and together, co-create something. It's not an "I-win-and-you-lose" world. It's a world where I need to think about how I can win and how I can make you win. The third kind of story we measure is when a group of staff have gone through the Empower program and then they organize a workshop for their peers… creating a culture of empowerment around them."

What impact has Empower had on helping Shell employees become better leaders?

Apte: "I think everybody is a leader and everybody strives to do the best they can. The Empower program, because it is based on breathing and meditation techniques, is a toolset that you walk away with and can practice every day. It's like running a marathon. You have to do the meditation practices every day to build your capacity to overcome the blocks to your own innovation and creativity. Secondly, regular meditation practice helps develop positive habits that will support you and the company to be creative and more innovative. I think Empower has provided these self-development tools to staff and empowered them to play a role in the innovation culture".

For more information on the leadership program that inspired the Empower program, refer to chapter 7, Tools for Inner Transformation —the TLEX Program (Transformational Leadership for Excellence). www.tlexprogram.com

Values and Ethics Permeating Organizations

More than ever before, we are socially conscious and aware of the implications of change on the mind and social interactions of others. This means we need to manage change in a way that is values-based, ethical, caring and empathetic. As leaders, we need to do the right things for people in the right way to encourage positive behaviors focused on developing a "win-win" attitude in the workplace.

Being values-based means decisions are driven and made with values in mind, consciously creating the future you want to experience. It is not making decisions based on past beliefs, actions, or behaviors. When decisions are made consciously and consistently this way, focusing on the new outcomes you want to achieve, they set a standard for new ways of behaving that people can model and trust. They provide an ethical basis for decision making the whole organization can follow.

Leaders must live the values at all times and align their personal values, beliefs, and behaviors to those they expect the organization to adopt and live as well. There needs to be a deep sense of coherence and alignment between the values of leadership and the organization.

Feedback is one value that is regularly required for a culture of continuous learning and improvement to develop. In most organization this is a difficult value to develop because it goes against a value many of us were raised with: "If you don't have something good to say, don't say anything at all." With this mindset and belief how do you develop the organization? What new skills or behaviors do managers and leaders need to shift this limiting perception to one that creates a positive experience of feedback? There needs to be a positive consequence to support change in behavior—one that is personal and answers the question, "What's in it for me." Most of us will not change unless there is some form of self-interest that is met.

When it comes to transforming culture, appreciating feedback as value-added is an example of the kind of mindset change leaders and employees need to be made aware of. What they are aware of and how they are thinking affects their behavior. With new consciousness and awareness they can choose different behavior. Developing new behaviors requires training your leaders and employees in new skills to give and receive feedback.

Once trained, leaders have to set the example by asking for feedback, then demonstrate the value this feedback has to them personally and to the organization as a whole. This requires leadership maturity, vulnerability, and authenticity in leading change.

Around the boardroom table, values and ethics are becoming an increasingly important topic of discussion. As social media and the Internet change the world of communications, leaders are challenged to live the value of authenticity in communication. Why is authentic communication so important? Honesty, openness, and transparency are key values in building trust relationships and product loyalty with customers. These are emotions, the soft stuff that is really the hard stuff to manage; leadership teams struggle to get past the fear of publicly disclosing their challenges with complex issues.

It takes courage for leaders and managers to face their fears and commit to organizational values of honesty, openness, and transparency. The results are often highly regarded by staff and customers. HR may fear honesty gives staff more to gripe about. The opposite is true. Employee engagement actually increases when leaders are humble and honest with them.

The reality is, "If we don't tell our story, others will tell it for us on social media." Stakeholders expect authentic communications that address the issues directly when difficult issues connected to the company are being debated.

How do you inculcate values-based, ethical behaviors in leadership, teams, and staff? Give them an experience of their true selves. At our core we share common human values. We all appreciate the values of compassion, caring, honesty, respect, love, and friendliness. Who would not want to be treated in this way?

If you were to ask employees for the leadership values they value the most, personal qualities that exhibit human values would predominate. These values create a positive, life-affirming, empowering, engaging, productive, and high-performing work environment. Ask employees what happens when human values are not present and opposite values such as manipulation, greed, blame, and control are demonstrated instead, and the answer is a stressful, frustrating, disengaged, low-performing work environment.

Worksheet 4-1 — Challenges in the Workplace

Purpose: To understand and explore the challenges in the workplace that impact performance and develop strategies for addressing workplace challenges.

Using the examples presented above, describe challenges in your work environment.
Give examples of how these affect you or your employees.
How was or is the problem being tackled?
Having read this chapter, do you have suggestions as to how you would engage staff in addressing the problem now?

Worksheet 4-2 — Values that Increase Performance

Purpose: To identify values that are an important source of energy and increase your performance.

Identify values in the corporate culture that attracted you to your current job.

How do you feel when you are able to live these values or they are appreciated by your manager and colleagues?

How do these values affect your level of engagement, creativity, and performance?

Have you ever left an organization because of how you were treated or because your strengths were not appreciated?

Chapter 5

Winds of Change

You cannot control what happens to you; you can, however, control your attitude toward it, and in that, you will be mastering change rather than allowing it to master you.

—Unknown

External forces affecting corporate culture

We are riding through the greatest period of change since the Industrial Revolution. These changes are affecting not only local communities and businesses, but entire societies around the globe. *"It's a small world after all."* The saying has never been truer and if the trend in globalization continues, it will feel like the world as we know it is shrinking.

Along with globalization, technology and workforce diversity are bringing us closer and changing how we work together. Technology such as Skype provides face-to-face meetings without the need to travel, and social media is changing how we market, communicate, and build relationships. With workforce diversity we now have multiple cultures and four generations working side by side, requiring a degree of awareness and respect for cultural sensitivities never experienced before. Expanding markets provide new opportunities for growth and development, products and services. Globalization has become a fixture for world commerce, greatly affecting the complexity of organizational culture and how people work together.

The starting point on your change journey is to understand your current reality and what is driving change in your business. Understanding what is driving change is critical to establishing the overall context within which cultural transformation occurs. The drivers are both external and internal. They are the impetus and motivation for change, providing the change effort's relevance and meaning. The drivers are the purpose for those leading the change as well as those who are going to be affected by the change.

When change is taking place, one thing you can be certain of is resistance. People typically do not like change, unless it is something they have chosen to change, like a new car or hairstyle. When the IT department decides to change your laptop or mobile device, change takes on a whole new complexion. Communication is crucial to minimizing resistance. People want to understand what is driving change and how the changes fit into the big picture, the organization's mission and vision. Having this information helps people to commit to it. The natural response to change underscores the importance of investing time at the front end of the change initiative to generate awareness and belongingness to build commitment. [13]

The model for change describes seven drivers for change—four that leaders are traditionally familiar with and three that are relatively new areas of focus. In figure 5-1 the familiar drivers move down from what is external and impersonal: environment, marketplace, business, and organization, to what is unfamiliar, internal, and personal: culture, behaviors, and values. Internal and personal drivers are rarely explored because they are intangible in nature and organizations find it hard to measure them.

---

13   Beyond Change Management, Copyright 2010, Dean Anderson and Linda Ackerman Anderson

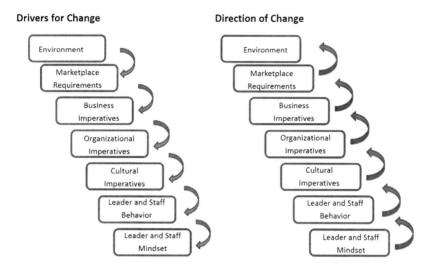

Figure 5-1—Drivers and Direction of Change

Environmental forces of change typically include: social, economic, political, governmental, technological, demographic, legal, and the natural environment.

Marketplace requirements reflect the customer needs and demands which arise from the environmental forces that are affecting them. For example new technology will create a rise in expectations of service levels, speed of delivery and innovation.

Business imperatives are the strategies companies must successfully implement to meet the market (customer) requirements. These changes can mean rethinking the mission and vision, new business models, products, services, and pricing. As the environment changes it has an impact on the customer requirements which in turn is reflected in the new strategies required to be adapt and be successful in meeting market demands.

Organizational imperatives are reflected in how the organization must evolve to successfully deliver on the new business strategies to meet market demands. Changes can be expected in the following: organizational structure, systems, processes, resources, technology, skills, leadership competencies, and staffing levels.

Cultural imperatives are the new ways of being and working together. Changes in the organization's structure, systems, processes, and management to meet new goals often mean changes in behavior that will require management training to ensure the staff are capable of delivering the desired results. Whenever new behaviors or skills are required to deliver on strategies this means the culture (how we do things) will be affected.

Leader and employee behavior must change to reflect the new culture and organizational structure to deliver on the business strategy to meet the needs of the marketplace due to changing environmental forces. Changes in behavior can include a different style of making decisions, frequency of collaborative dialogue with staff and stakeholders, and tone in communicating. In order for the culture to change leaders must role model the change they want to see and walk the talk for staff.

Leader and employee mindset is the collective set of beliefs, values, assumptions which are the driving force for our behavior. The first step in the change process is to become aware of what beliefs and assumptions are driving behavior. Once we know what they are we are more in control of how we can choose to change our behavior. "If you continue to think as you have always thought, then you will continue to get what you have always got".[14]New information that is gained from doing an environmental scan and understanding the external forces can lead to shift in mindset. A shift in mindset can be a catalyst for new ideas and new strategies to meet the organizational and business imperatives. This shift is also what is required for staff to understand the compelling reasons for change and behave differently to support the new strategies and achieve different results.

The most challenging struggles identified during change deal with leaders' and team members' need to develop awareness, ownership, and responsibility for the internal drivers of change such as personal behaviors and values. This is because organizations do not change: it is the people in them that do. For sustained success and real change to happen, the change must begin at the base, in the mindset and values of leaders and staff. When mindsets change, new thinking and strategies emerge, making new behaviors possible, sparking a rippling effect up the drivers of change.

Change is a constant companion in our modern world, and it is coming at us faster and faster. The changes are affecting us both in ways we know and in ways we are not aware of. Because these changes influence all parts of society and,

---

14   Marilyn Ferguson, The Aquarian Conspiracy (1987)

ultimately our lives, we have no choice but to keep pace with them and learn how to adapt. Change is the new normal.

An example of the rapidly changing environment and encompassing globalization is the constantly growing and changing telecommunications market. Telephones in the 1980s were dependent on landlines. During the last few decades mobile phones have become common accessories available to the general public and consumers of all ages, including technology-savvy two-year-olds swiping and accessing their favorite video or music. During the last five years the development of smartphones has caused a revolution in the telecommunications world. Mobile applications are now the way business-to-consumer products and services are being marketed and sold.

Every day new technology is being released and manufacturers are going out of business. We used to wait before investing in the next laptop or cellphone, but now advancements are so much the norm that this strategy doesn't work any longer. We are more likely to follow the developments online, dependent on the newer technology and software to decide when and what to invest in. If you want to be competitive in the modern world, you cannot afford to procrastinate and not renew your technology before investing in the next generation of hardware and software.

An example of this is social media. The world is connected by Twitter, LinkedIn and Facebook to market effectively, develop brand presence and trust, connect and communicate with consumers, professionals, colleagues, friends, and family. These new technologies are affecting every strategic plan developed in the last three years and taking up a lot of time in boardroom discussions. They are influencing why, what, how and when leaders communicate messages to the general public.

With globalization and the speed of the Internet to share information, technology is having an impact on how open and transparent corporations need to be, and how they will control the flow of information or have others do it for them. This is increasing the need and importance to have shared values and behaviors, especially on the leadership team, to assist in the decision-making process.

In 2008, Maple Leaf Foods had an outbreak of listeriosis in Canada linked to cold cuts from a Maple Leaf meat plant in Toronto, Ontario. Twenty-two people died and there were fifty-seven total confirmed cases. Within a very short time Michael McCain, the CEO of Maple Leaf Foods, faced the cameras and microphones and made sure he was seen and heard to be involved, concerned, compassionate, and focused on fixing the problem. McCain set the gold standard for how to deal with a communication crisis. The values of the Maple Leaf leadership team facilitated a speedy decision-making process that helped the company survive the crisis.

In our modern society, the exponential increases in risk, uncertainty and fear are affecting our mindsets and values. There is a negative belief about globalization—that it is the reason people are losing their jobs, making the job market tougher, tighter, competitive, and life more difficult to meet the basic needs of security and survival. The increase in terrorism is also affecting our mindsets and values, challenging our values of acceptance and appreciation of diversity with regard to the immigrant populations who are invited to live and work in our communities.

Here are just a few statistics as to how the world has changed since the 1900s. Acts of terrorism:

- 1900—49, eleven
- 1950—70, fifty
- 1970s—thirteen per year (129)
- 1980s—nineteen per year (190)
- 1990s—twenty per year (205)
- 2000s—142 per year (one every 2.5 days)

Another of modern society's realities is the depletion of earth's resources. Two aspects of this problem are source and sink. Typically, we consider depletion of earth's resources as shortages of raw materials, such as fossil fuels, basic minerals, topsoil, freshwater, and forests (source). But depletion of earth's resources has its consequences in climate change, prolonged heat waves, droughts, ocean acidification, and production of toxics (sink). Whether the depletion of resources is due to overpopulation or not, the fact remains that since the 1500s a total of 875 species have become extinct. [15]

---

15 See for more information on resource depletion: http://monthlyreview.org/2013/01/01/global-resource-depletion , read on April 8, 2013

Our modern society is currently using between 1.3 to 1.5 times the earth's resources. What this means is we are using the earth's resources more rapidly than they can be regenerated—especially the renewable resources like fresh water, fish, and plants [16] The World Wildlife Fund (WWF)[17] estimates the earth's resources will be depleted by 2050.

A fundamental problem is that business believes the planet is there to serve the economy instead of economics serving the planet.

The financial crisis of 2008 was caused by pure greed made worse by the concentrated power in stock exchanges around the globe. As a result, the rich are getting richer and poor are getting poorer. The protest movement Occupy Wall Street (OWS) began on September 17, 2011, in Zuccotti Park, located in New York City's Wall Street financial district and spread to Occupy protests and movements around the world. OWS raised issues of social and economic inequality, greed, corruption, and the perceived undue influence of corporations on government—particularly from the financial services sector. The OWS slogan *"We are the 99%"* refers to income inequality and wealth distribution in the U.S. between the wealthiest 1% and the rest of the population.

Rising CEO salaries and severance benefit plans that are over 350 times the average salary in corporations point to the inequality that exists in the corporate world. On November 24, 2013, Swiss voters weighed in on a referendum that would pass legislation to cap the pay of top executives at no more than twelve times the lowest-paid workers in their companies.[18] The so-called 1:12 initiative for Fair Pay was an attempt to narrow a growing wage gap in one of the world's wealthiest nations and would have meant big pay cuts for business leaders. A youth wing of the Social Democrats gathered the 100,000 signatures needed to force a nationwide vote. However, the referendum did not pass.

Looking at the current reality, we have to conclude that 2.5 million years of evolution will end if we don't care for the life support system of our

---

16   See article http://www.northeastern.edu/news/2012/05/biodiversity/ , read on April 8, 2013

17   See for example the World Wildlife Fund (WWF) footprint report on http://www. footprintnetwork.org/images/uploads/lpr2002.pdf , read on April 8, 2013.

18   http://www.cbc.ca/news/business/swiss-vote-may-cap-ceo-pay-at-12x-lowest-worker-s-salary-1.2435505

planet earth. The younger generation of leaders understands the need to shift from "me' to "we" in mindsets, values, and behaviors. Now it is time for *all* generations of leaders to join in the change: to let go of limiting beliefs and fears; to expand their sense of self and identity; and to develop a more inclusive view of society—a view that includes a sense of corporate and social responsibility that contributes to society and is good for all stakeholders, not just themselves and their immediate corporate family—to see how they can be the best *for* the world not just *in* the world.

With the rise in terrorism, increases in unemployment, and increases in cultural diversity, it is no surprise we need to make a concerted effort to reduce the levels of stress, violence, and anxiety these changes are creating in society. Lamenting about how awful things are now compared to ten or twenty years ago and wishing the world would revert back to the way life used to be, is not going to change things. So how do we help ourselves?

Changing how we think, look, and feel about the challenges is one way. We can reduce our personal levels of stress and increase our feelings of harmony by accepting what is happening around us and respecting cultural diversity—if I can accept a person or situation and respect the differences, my mind and emotions are more at peace and I can respond instead of reacting to what is happening around me. This creates the mental and emotional space and opportunity for new ideas and new solutions to surface and become reality.

Necessity for new levels of consciousness

The significant problems we face cannot be solved with the same level of thinking that created them.

—Albert Einstein

In order to bring about the needed changes to solve our global challenges, we need to lift and shift our level of thinking and raise our awareness to a new level of consciousness. So how do we open minds, shift mindsets, increase our awareness, and create a new consciousness to see things differently and find new strategies to solve our global challenges?

We need:

- new belief structures to solve the problems facing the planet
- new dialogue on sharing resources
- a rethinking of well-being at a global level

This is a tall order considering the current state of global political affairs. Of all the nations in the world, the Nordic countries are the most advanced and ready in terms of their national values of equality and cooperation in solving social problems. Unless the basic human needs of a country are met it is too difficult for nations to think about sharing and creating common visions with other nation states. The same is true within teams and between corporations looking to partner and collaborate.

The Nordic countries have been successful at meeting the basic needs by creating a welfare model based on a shared political goal of encouraging strong social cohesion. The Nordic social model is renowned for the universal nature of its welfare provision, which is based on the core values of equal opportunities, social solidarity, and security for all. The model promotes social rights and the principle that everyone is entitled to equal access to social and health services, education and culture.

A central goal of the model is to create opportunities for all to take part in the social life and in the decision-making process in society. The Nordic model is characterised by strong ties between welfare and labor-market policy. The welfare system is mainly funded by taxes, which are relatively high in the region, to support the social programs.

The Nordic countries are relatively well off compared to the rest of Europe. The levels of employment and flexibility on the Nordic labor market are high, as are the birth rates. Comprehensive and financially affordable child-minding services and care of the elderly enable women.

The educational school system is based on the same values of equality and cooperation with remarkable results. The following case study takes a look at the small Nordic country of Finland.

Case Study – Finland's Educational System

Finland used to be known as the home of Nokia, the mobile phone giant. But lately Finland has been attracting attention on global surveys for quality of life. *Newsweek* declared it number one in its 2010 analysis and Finland's national education system has been receiving particular praise, because in recent years Finnish students have been turning in some of the highest test scores in the world.

Finland's schools score consistently at the top of world rankings, yet the pupils have the fewest number of class hours in the developed world. The Finnish philosophy with education is that everyone has something to contribute and those who struggle in certain subjects should not be left behind. The Scandinavian country is considered an education superpower because it values equality more than excellence.

Finland's schools owe their newfound fame primarily to one study: the PISA survey, conducted every three years by the Organization for Economic Co-operation and Development (OECD). The survey compares fifteen-year-olds in different countries in reading, math, and science. Finland has ranked at or near the top in all three competencies on every survey since 2000, neck and neck with super achievers such as South Korea and Singapore.

Children in Finland only start main school at age seven. The idea is that before then they learn best when they're playing and by the time they finally get to school they are keen to start learning. Less is more. Finnish parents obviously claim some credit for the impressive school results. There is a culture of reading with the kids at home and families have regular contact with their children's teachers. Teaching standards are high in Finland, where teaching is a prestigious career and teachers are highly valued. The educational system's success in Finland seems to be part cultural. Pupils study in a relaxed and informal atmosphere.

Compared with the East Asian model of long hours of studying and memorization, Finland's success is particularly intriguing because Finnish schools give less homework and engage children in more creative play. This has led to foreign delegations making trips to Finland to visit schools and talk with the nation's education experts.

One of the most significant things about the Finnish school system is that the country has no private schools. Only a small number of independent schools exist, and even they are all publicly financed; none can charge tuition fees. There are no private universities, either. This means that practically every person in Finland attends public school, whether for pre-K or a Ph.D.

The thinking being… "If education is expensive, try ignorance."

The obsession with competition and excellence in our own schools leads to performance tracking through regular testing and accountability for bad teachers or merit pay for good teachers. This runs contrary to Finland where there are no standardized tests. Instead, the public school system's teachers are trained to assess children in classrooms using independent tests they create themselves. All children receive a report card at the end of each semester, but these reports are based on individualized grading by each teacher. Periodically, the Ministry of Education tracks national progress by testing a few sample groups across a range of different schools.

As for accountability of teachers and administrators, there is no word for accountability in Finnish. Accountability is something that is left when responsibility has been subtracted.

What matters in Finland is that all teachers and administrators are given prestige, decent pay, and a lot of responsibility. A master's degree is required to enter the profession and teacher training programs are among the most selective professional schools in the country. If a teacher is bad, it is the principal's responsibility to notice and deal with it.

And while our society loves competition, nothing makes Finns more uncomfortable. Pasi Sahlberg, director of the Finnish Ministry of Education's Center for International Mobility and author of the new book *Finnish Lessons: What Can the World Learn from Educational Change in Finland?* quotes a line from Finnish writer Samuli Paronen: "Real winners do not compete." There are no lists of best schools or teachers in Finland. The main driver of education policy is not competition between teachers and between schools, but cooperation.

Decades ago when the Finnish school system was badly in need of reform, the goal of the program that Finland instituted, resulting in so much success today, was never excellence—it was equity. Since the 1980s, the main driver of Finnish education policy has been the idea that every child should have exactly the same opportunity to learn, regardless of family background, income, or geographic location. Education has been seen first and foremost not as a way to produce star performers, but as an instrument to even out social inequality.

In the Finnish view, this means that schools should be healthy, safe environments for children. This approach starts with the basics. Finland offers all pupils free school meals, easy access to health care, psychological counselling, and individualized student guidance.

Since academic excellence wasn't a particular priority on the Finnish to-do list, when Finland's students scored so high on the first PISA survey in 2001, many Finns thought the results must be a mistake. But subsequent PISA tests confirmed that Finland was producing academic excellence through its particular policy focus on equity.

This policy seems especially poignant now, after the financial crisis and Occupy Wall Street. The chasm between those who can afford private school tuition of $35,000 per child per year, or even just the price of a house in a good public school district, and the other "99 percent" is obvious to see.

The questions of size or homogeneity are not reason to dismiss the Finnish example. Finland *is* a relatively homogeneous country. As of 2010, only 4.6 % of Finnish residents had been born in another country, compared with 12.7 % in the United States. But the number of foreign-born residents in Finland doubled during the decade leading up to 2010, and the country did not lose its edge in education. Immigrants tended to concentrate in certain areas, causing some schools to become much more mixed than others, yet there has not been much change in the remarkable lack of variation between Finnish schools in the PISA surveys across the same period.

Samuel Abrams, a visiting scholar at Columbia University's Teachers College, has addressed[19] the effects of size and homogeneity on a nation's education performance by comparing Finland with another Nordic country: Norway. Like Finland, Norway is small and not especially diverse overall, but unlike Finland it has taken an approach to education that is more American than Finnish. The result: mediocre performance in the PISA survey. It seems that educational policy is more important to the success of a country's school system than the nation's size or ethnic makeup.

When Finnish policymakers needed to reform the country's education system in the 1970s, they decided to invest in a knowledge-based economy because they realized to be competitive, Finland could not rely on manufacturing or its limited natural resources.

---

19 http://www.newrepublic.com/article/politics/82329/education-reform-Finland-US

Through Finland's experience we see it is possible to create equality. And perhaps even more important, Finland's experience shows that it is possible to achieve excellence by focusing not on competition, but on cooperation, and not on choice, but on equity.

The problem facing our society isn't the ethnic diversity of the population but the economic inequality of society and this is the problem that Finnish education reform addressed. More equity in our society might just be what is needed to be more competitive abroad.

The challenge is changing how we think about our problems. Change is possible if we shift our level of thinking, awareness, and consciousness.

"When President Kennedy was making his appeal for advancing American science and technology by putting a man on the moon by the end of the 1960's, many said it couldn't be done. But he had a dream. Just like Martin Luther King a few years later had a dream. Those dreams came true. Finland's dream was that it wanted to have good public education for every child regardless of where they go to school or what kind of families they come from, and many even in Finland said it couldn't be done."[20]

Until deficiency needs are met, countries, organizations and individuals cannot think about evolving to higher levels of development. Deficiency needs are:

- security—satisfying physiological needs of survival to keep our bodies alive and healthy
- relationships—satisfying emotional need for belonging and being loved
- self-esteem—satisfying the need to feel good about yourself and feel respected by others

Based on what we now know about the current reality, it is time to focus on how to change this reality into a more productive and sustainable reality. It is only through this change that we can achieve evolution and transformation. But for evolution and transformation to happen, we need to unlearn and create space into which new wisdom can come. We need to let go of old ways and beliefs to make way for the new. The needed changes can be frightening. Change creates

---

20   http://www.theatlantic.com/national/archive/2011/12/what-americans-keep-ignoring-about-finlands-school-success/250564/

fear because of the expected losses we might think we will suffer. The question then becomes: What are we afraid of losing?

> *The act of discovery consists not in finding new lands, but in seeing with new eyes.*
>
> **—Marcel Proust**

Leading change starts first with effectively leading change in you. What are some things you can do to accomplish this and create space for new wisdom?

Take time to make a list of all the things you can let go of:

Worksheet 5-1 — Letting Go

Item	Not needed	Less necessary

Collaboration and Interdependency

In the Nordic model we saw the role and impact the values of cooperation and equality have had on creating a healthy and successful society. These are high levels of consciousness to which the rest of the world can aspire. With the complexity of life inside and outside organizations increasing, the values of collaboration and interdependency are becoming necessary in how we think and how we work together and partner with public, private, and non-profit sectors to find solutions. No one person, team or organization has all the answers any more.

Collaboration and interdependency are new ways of thinking and acting to solve our global challenges. The external drivers of change are requiring us to act and take responsibility in new ways that have not been thought of before. These external forces of change are creating new internal forces affecting the culture inside organizations and the norms of behavior and values of their leaders. The change needs to begin at the level of thinking and consciousness of the leaders. When leaders change how they see the world and change their perspective on how they view a problem and see it instead as an opportunity, whole new strategies can emerge. This is why in figure 5-1, the direction of change begins at the bottom, with a change in mindset.

Young leaders see potential in globalization and partnering to drive convergence in public, private, and non-profit sectors to find solutions to the world's toughest problems. These emerging leaders were raised with different values than graduates thirty years ago, who were raised in families where children were seen and not heard. The emerging leaders were invited constantly as they were growing up to participate, collaborate, and take responsibility in decision making. Their passions are more global with a social mindset and belief in working collaboratively to share information and learn from each other.

Information is doubling approximately every eleven hours on the Internet. This volume does not include information from the people we work with or our partners. The amount of available data and sources of business intelligence becomes staggering when considering all that is at hand to solve the complex problems with which we are confronted. The real challenges arise when we need to work collaboratively to share our experience and knowledge. Working collaboratively is a big change for many leaders. It takes a high degree of trust to work effectively together and an investment by the leader to build internal cohesion on the leadership team.

What would your reaction be if I were to say to you, "*You now need to collaborate and partner with your competitor?*" Wouldn't this raise the hairs on the back of your neck, create a feeling of fear in your gut, and kick all your defenses into high gear?

To change your behavior and start partnering with a person, team, or organization that you previously considered a competitor, there would have to be very compelling reasons to change your mindset and behaviors. You would truly have to respect and trust the source of the request, and be sold on why it's a good idea, to overcome your emotional reactions. Your value system, how you think and feel, your attitudes and beliefs would have to change to support a change in your behavior.

Our fears exist primarily in the levels of consciousness related to security, relationships, and self-esteem. We need to learn how to manage and master these fears if we want to realize our full potential. The first step is to seek to understand the origin of the fear that it is triggering the fear response. With understanding and awareness, these fears often dissipate and turn out to be not as large as we first thought. With self-awareness and courage we learn how to respond instead of reacting, and gain new confidence in the success we achieve.

Effective collaboration depends on team members being able to trust and commit to each other. Any fears, doubts, or obstacles need to be addressed by having the courage to discuss the potential barriers to success. If the vision is long-term interdependency for the successful delivery of products or services, team members have to develop the level of trust and cohesion this level of relationship requires. Taking the time to get to know one another by creating a strategic plan together will have the desired effect of forging this level of trust and commitment.

The Technology of Participation (ToP®) strategic planning method is one such process that yields very effective results in building trust-based committed implementation teams. A key element in the process is the selection of stakeholders. It is recommended to invite the right sub-group of stakeholders from across the organization. The stakeholders invited will become your champions going forward after the planning process. Choose your stakeholders with the intention of building a support team and working groups that will assist in implementing the strategic plan. The same stakeholders participate in

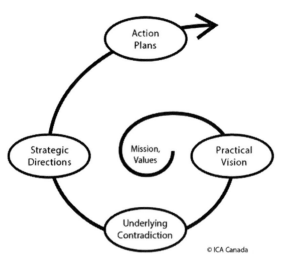

Figure 5-2 – Technology of Participation Strategic Planning Process

all the workshops. This provides continuity and maximizes the results. Having the right stakeholders participate in creating the vision and strategies ensures that whoever reads the plan will be able to see themselves in the results. This helps enormously when sharing and communicating your mission, mandate and vision.

The process includes:

1. **Mission and Purpose:** Answers the question "What is our purpose?"
   a. Defining the mission and writing a mission statement articulates the project's/initiative's intention and connects to the personal sense of purpose.
   b. This connection will give the group enhanced motivation, commitment, and fulfillment.
   c. Sound strategy is not enough; it must be founded upon a clearly stated mission that is understood by all members of an organization.
2. **Practical Vision:** *What will the successful project/initiative look like upon completion?*
   a. The idea is to create a concrete vision of the project /initiative together with key stakeholders whose support and commitment are critical to success.
   b. It will be based on images of the future.
   c. The workshop method will bring to the surface many individual visions into one conscious picture.
   d. Every stakeholder has a piece of the puzzle. No one has the whole picture until the group creates it together.
3. **Underlying Contradiction or Obstacles:**
   a. Critical analysis pinpoints to what might prevent the project from achieving the vision.
   b. Examples include constraints such as behaviors, values, systems, or policies that are currently in place and will need to be addressed.
   c. The blocks to the vision are identified, including what is being blocked and how it is being blocked.
4. **Strategic Directions (Approaches):**
   a. Once the obstacles are understood, solutions or doorways to achieving the vision naturally emerge.

    b. Strategies, approaches or key focus areas of activity are developed that will enable the vision to come into being.

    c. The strategies will have a wide span of involvement to engage key stakeholders, and serve as a communication vehicle for the vision, to develop a deeper awareness for the need to change.

5. Goals and Action Plan:

    a. A short-term plan is created with measurable outcomes and goals for each strategy.

    b. Each strategy has a timeline with specific actions or initiatives that engages management, staff, and clients to build awareness, commitment for change, and identifies roles and responsibilities where appropriate.

    c. The implementation time frame is usually within the next 12 months, and will need to be revisited to reflect on what is working well and where improvements or more focus need to be made.

6. Values and Behaviors:

    a. Values along with desired behaviors for each value need to be identified that will support the successful achievement of the strategies.

    b. Create a plan of action to develop, manage, and evaluate ongoing progress towards developing conscious competency in living the values and behaviors.

    c. Personal alignment of leaders to ensure they are "walking the talk" and serving as role models for the new values.

    d. Review existing systems and processes to ensure alignment and provide necessary training or make changes where needed.

7. Articulate compelling reasons for change

    a. When new values and behaviors are being introduced into an existing organization, team members and the organizations will need to discuss and identify the compelling reasons for change.

    b. Explore how the project/initiative will remain adaptable, continue to learn and grow, and build long-term resilience into management practices.

Building a collaborative interdependent team takes trustworthy leadership, common values, and a community spirit. Facilitative leadership skills focus on ensuring team members and diverse stakeholders continue to learn and grow from each other. There will be plenty of opportunity to build stronger trust relationships as different situations arise while the strategies and action plan are carried out.

There are twelve basic conditions that must be met to create a climate of trust. These are shown in the Trust Matrix below[21]. Teams must master all these components to create a high-performing leadership team and a high-performing organization.

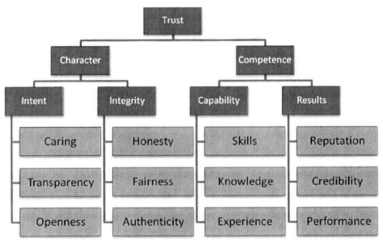

Figure 5-3—Trust Matrix

Intent
> **Caring**: To look out for the well-being of the organization and all its employees.
> **Transparency**: To be clear about the motivations that lie behind all decision making.
> **Openness**: To be accepting and receptive to the ideas and opinions of all employees.

Integrity
> **Honesty**: To be truthful and frank in all interpersonal communications.

---

21   Annex 10, *The Values-Driven Organization: Unleashing Human Potential for Performance and Profit*, by Richard Barrett, 2014

Fairness: To act without bias, discrimination, or injustice towards all employees.

Authenticity: To be consistent and sincere in thought, word, and action at all times.

Capability

Skills: To accomplish professional tasks with ease, speed, and proficiency.

Knowledge: To be very familiar with and conversant in a specific topic or professional subject matter.

Experience: To accumulate practical knowledge through personal observation.

Results

Reputation: To be held in favorable esteem by bosses, peers, and subordinates.

Credibility: To consistently articulate ideas in a convincing and believable manner.

Performance: To discharge personal responsibilities with accomplishment and excellence.

To be successful in collaborating and creating interdependency will require a high level of trust and internal cohesion on the leadership team. Internal cohesion begins with the leadership team. If the leadership team is out of alignment with each other, the whole organization will be at odds with itself, and cultural entropy will be high.

We have found that the biggest single success factor in building a high performance organization is creating a cohesive leadership team. We have also found this to be the factor that organizations struggle with the most.

Case Study: World Forum for Ethics in Business—Leadership Forum

The International Leadership Symposium on Ethics in Business is an annual event taking place in the European Parliament in Brussels and its satellite conferences. This forum brings together leaders from business, politics, academia, civil society, and faith-based organizations to discuss new leadership styles that support inclusive and sustainable development and ensure profitability for businesses. It provides a platform for leading minds to share experiences and expertise on the value of an ethics-based approach to deal with today's challenges in the global markets. It also examines the impact of this ethical approach on the bottom line.

The most recent forum took place in June 2013, in Geneva, Switzerland. The International Leadership Symposium on Ethics in Business is an initiative of The World Forum for Ethics in Business, a registered public interest foundation with the aim to pursue and establish ethical foundations of business in a globalized world.

The Conference in Geneva was a satellite conference held for the first time at the United Nations and organized in partnership with Global Partnerships Forum. The Global Partnerships Forum (GPF) brings together policy makers, business leaders, entrepreneurs, philanthropists, investors, and thought leaders from across sectors to address global challenges. The GPF aims to move the needle from aid to investments, using the power of partnerships. For more information, visit the website: www.Partnerships.org.

The World Forum for Ethics in Business was organized in Geneva in 2013 in cooperation with:

- International Association for Human Values (IAHV)
- The World Bank Institute
- Global Partnerships Forum

The Conference considered the following questions:

- What are the qualities of good governance?
- The importance of transparency?
- Business and Ethics – Complementary or Contradictory values?
- Leadership in the 21st Century – Time for a Paradigm Shift?
- In the wake of the economic crisis, is globalization still beneficial to society at large? In this next phase of globalization, who are the winners and who are the losers? How can globalization serve as a means to distribute wealth in a more equitable way?
- What is the role of the global organization in addressing poverty, improving education and health systems, and dealing with unemployment and environmental degradation?
- What practices contribute to the highest executive and organizational performance?

- How can organizations implement an ethics-based approach to transforming society and contributing to a better sense of community at the global level, while being profitable and achieving long-term success?
- Leaders share their secrets to sustainability and success!

In 1997, when Ted Turner committed $1 billion to support UN causes, it became clear that the needs of the underprivileged require multiple constituencies to collaborate in support of common goals. This was the genesis of the *Multi-Stakeholder Partnerships Model:* using the expertise of the private sector, leadership of the public sector, and successful delivery mechanisms of civil society.

Initiatives such as the Global Partnerships Forum are a unique opportunity to **develop high-impact collaborations.** These innovative partnerships promote economic growth and foster greater prosperity around the world.

The challenges are enormous, as are the opportunities. Using the power of collaborative partnerships, social change is possible. You are invited to join this collective effort and contribute your expertise and engagement.

To build collaborative partnerships access
bonus facilitated planning resources by becoming a member at:
www.CultureLeadershipGroup.com

Worksheet 5-2 — Shifting Mindsets

Purpose: To develop an understanding for the compelling reasons for change that create a shift in mindset and values, and foster new ways of thinking which will lead to new strategies and opportunities.

Conduct an environmental scan of your organization by identifying the drivers for change in referring to figure 5-3.

What environmental forces external to your organization are driving change?

What new requirements are your customers demanding?

What new business strategies are necessary to meet your customer requirements?

How do you need to change your systems, processes, structures, roles, or technology to successfully implement the business strategies?

How does your culture need to change to support the organizational requirements?

How does leadership and staff need to shift their behavior to support these cultural changes?

Leaders:

Staff:

How does leadership and staff need to shift their mindsets and values to make these behavioral changes?

Leaders:

Staff:

What is scary about the changes that are being asked for? What is surprising? What is exciting?

What new ways of thinking or acting are required? How will this affect your business, existing vision and strategies?

What's one thing you can do differently tomorrow that will lead to changing how you think and work with others?

Chapter 6

Navigating Rough Seas

One of the biggest challenges is creating the right environment for people to speak out, so they know they're safe and can speak openly and honestly.

Stressed and Burned Out

The impacts from the "winds of change" can be seen in the headlines of major publications across North America. They are a result of an increasingly fast pace and global business environment:

- *How to keep staff motivated during layoffs and pay cuts*
- Stress stifles creativity and innovation needed for economic growth and competitiveness
- *Investing in innovation is crucial to economic growth and competiveness*

Figure 6-1—Recent Headlines in Major Publications

- Employees are dissatisfied with pay raises and bonus; they think they are not enough
- *Increased numbers and speed of activities, increase in performance goals, shortened innovation cycles, new management technologies and organizational systems. These succeed for a while until the CEO tries to make the furious pace the new normal. The burst of achievement becomes chronic overload with negative consequences. This overload saps employee motivation and energy. The company's focus is scattered in various directions that confuse the clients and employees and brand*
- Market pressures lead to CEOs taking on more than they can handle

Imagine for a moment you are an employee of a firm that has been acquired in a merger. The principle aim of the merger was to increase shareholder wealth by managing financial resources—people, processes and projects—more efficiently and reducing costs. It's Sunday night and the feeling of dread and anxiety is beginning to creep into your belly. The thought of going into work Monday morning and facing the conflict-ridden work environment is bringing on this physical sensation. As much as you try to think positive thoughts, your gut is tightening and you know you are in for another sleepless night. You wonder how much more you can take.

When you manage to drag yourself out of bed and into work, exhausted from waking up every hour, your level of enthusiasm and engagement is low.

With all the change happening around you, you know there is so much more you'd like to contribute; however, the work environment and management style does not recognize, enable, or value what you have to offer. You're a creative person, yet your ideas are not being asked for. You like to have fun, but with all the layoffs there aren't many smiles going around. You have given up hope of trying to make a difference.

Job insecurity is a concern. Last month two people on your team were let go. You know times are tough, still the fear of losing your job is affecting your ability to think creatively and relate effectively with others. Instead of putting the company and team first or thinking creatively about how to deliver excellent customer service, you are thinking about how to protect your job and make sure you meet your target deliverables. Forget management's mantra of "all for one and one for all." They don't seem to be living this value or doing everything possible to prevent people from being laid off.

Along with losing valuable team members, you have lost relationships and friendships with people who were family to you. It feels like part of your heart has been ripped out and you are half a person. There is a feeling of loss and mourning in the office that no one dares to speak about. Heads are buried in the work. Yet the feeling of loss is there in every meeting like an elephant sitting in the middle of the table.

Morale is so low it's hard to find any excitement or will to actively engage with others. Effective teamwork and collaboration are non-existent. No one trusts each other. People around you are doing the same as you, hoarding information and protecting their turf. It's hard to focus on work because your energy level is so low.

Mental clarity is non-existent. Your thoughts are constantly vacillating between the past and the future, regret and anxiety. Coffee breaks are a highlight in the day, to pump your system with caffeine and meet with colleagues. The main topic of conversation is complaining about how bad things are and how much fun it used to be. If feels good to get things off your chest and blame others for the current malaise, but at the end of the conversation you don't feel any better; in fact, you feel worse.

Management is asking staff to be patient and understanding while the changes are taking place. You have worked for the company a long time and have ideas that would help reduce costs and apply the changes that are being rolled out. The only problem is management does not seem to want to listen and hear your ideas. The change strategies are coming down from above. Senior leadership is making decisions without consultation or collaboration with staff. They believe they know best what is good for the business without input from those at the grassroots level that actually do the work.

The new management systems and processes that are being rolled out require training and development of new competencies on top of existing workloads. Overtime has become the new norm. Expertise that defined your reputation and gave you job satisfaction is no longer valued or needed. Information and decisions once under your control are being taken away and given to others. New skills and capabilities are valued over job seniority. New roles and responsibilities are being given to younger employees who do not know the organization or its history. The strengths you have acquired over the years are not being valued or recognized.

Do parts of this scenario look familiar to you? These workplace stressors are playing out all across organizations today. The winds of change in our current reality are creating a crisis in society. There is a feeling of darkness and loss of hope. Prices are high and people feel insecure. Addictions have increased. The sale of alcohol is increasing. Kids are getting addicted to more harmful drugs. There is an increase in suicides. Stress and burnout are on the rise, with anxiety and depression seriously affecting employee health, the ability to perform and contribute productively. We need a wave of change.

The pace of change is a significant factor in the current levels of stress. Instability, downsizing and constant change in organizations are failing to provide employees with the security, relationships, and self-esteem they need in their lives to feel healthy, balanced, and productive.

Leadership is another factor. Leaders are having a hard time providing a clear sense of direction and purpose. During change, employees want information to know where the organization is going, and how they are going to get there. They want to feel connected to a sense of mission and purpose that will inspire them. Often leaders can't provide this direction because they themselves are not in a position themselves to know the answer. The global marketplace is so volatile that month to month they have to react to external pressures and make decisions without providing sufficient communications to staff. Failure to provide engaging communications effectively is a limiting factor that is creating a feeling of distrust between management and staff. Without trust, leading an organization through change is difficult and adds more work to the change effort.

The following stressors affect the organization's ability to navigate in a desired direction. If the engine of a ship is not in peak performance, it will affect the power, speed and resilience of the ship to respond in emergencies and adapt to the changes in the ocean around it.

Table 6-1 — Stressors in the Workplace

Categories of Job Stressors	Examples of Sources of Stress
Leadership	• Controlling—imposes will on others • Risk averse, fear of failure • Not collaborative • Autocratic and directive • Unilateral decision making, not building consensus • Blaming others, not taking personal responsibility • Arrogant • Cautious, not trusting others • Driven by greed and profit • Two sets of values, one for senior managers, one for staff

Work-life balance	• Toxic success – driven to succeed • Self-doubt, "I am not good enough" • Sense of obligation • Role responsibility conflicts • Increase in performance goals with no reduction in priorities • Long hours • Family exposed to work-related hazards
Organizational structure/culture	• Risk intolerant • Increase in numbers and speed of activities • New management technology and organizational systems • Loss of power, non-participation in decision making • Controlling management style • Poor communication patterns or information flow • Lack of systems in workplace to respond to concerns • Not engaging employees when undergoing organizational change • Perceived lack of fairness • Loss of control over information, work and projects • Misalignment of personal and organizational values • Bureaucracy, hierarchy, silo mentality, internal competition • Lack of competency, need for new capabilities to perform new role • Lack of trust in leadership, past history is cause for concern

Factors unique to the job	• Over- or under-worked • information overload • Pace, variety, and meaningfulness of work • Lack of autonomy—ability to make own decisions about job or tasks • Shift work, long hours, training preparation, lack of appreciation, environment, isolation
Role in organization	• Conflicting job demands • Multiple supervisors • Lack of clarity in responsibilities or expectations
Career development	• Under/over promotion • Job security—fear of redundancy from the economy or lack of work to do • Lack of development opportunities • Overall job satisfaction
Relationships at work (Interpersonal)	• Conflicts or lack of support from supervisors or co-workers • Sub-ordinates • Threat of violence, harassment • Lack of trust • Lack of systems to deal with unacceptable behavior

Looking at the number of things that cause stress in the workplace, it's easy to see how they might cause stress and conflict, causing people to disengage and seek employment elsewhere.

Lost Productivity

Yes, stress does have an impact on the overall health and performance of your organization. It comes from many different places, from too much to do and not enough time in which to do it. Our mental, physical, emotional, and spiritual parts of our selves are stretched beyond our limits due to situations outside of our control. It can affect both employees and employers alike.

Some stress is normal. In fact, it is often what provides us with the energy and motivation to meet our daily challenges. Stress in these situations helps us rise to the occasion and meet our deadlines, sales or production targets, or find new clients. Some people would not consider this type of challenge stress because having met the challenge we feel satisfied and happy.

Our bodies are pre-programmed with a set of automatic responses to deal with stress. When faced with an immediate stressful situation our "fight or flight" response kicks in. The problem is that our bodies deal with all types of stress in the same way. When experiencing stress for long periods of time, such as constant stressors at work, this system does not get a chance to turn off and relax.

The physical effects of prolonged stress include[22]:

- increased blood pressure
- increased metabolism (faster heartbeat, faster respiration)
- decrease in protein synthesis and digestion
- decrease in immune response systems
- increased cholesterol
- localized inflammation (redness, swelling, heat and pain)
- increased stomach acids

There are many signs and symptoms that can indicate someone is having difficulty coping with the amount of stress they are experiencing on the job (See table 6.2 on next page):

When people express these emotions or engage in these behaviors, productivity drops and there can be an increase in potentially harmful accidents. Performance is reduced on jobs requiring hand-eye or foot-eye coordination; poor judgment and errors in decision making increase. People may put their bodies under more physical stress than normal, increasing the potential for serious harm. Change is a root cause for stress, especially if the change is being done to us and we have not had any input into the change.

---

22   Basic Certification Training Program: Participant Manual, Copyright 2006 by the Workplace Safety and Insurance Board of Ontario

Table 6-2 — Signs and Symptoms of Difficulties Coping

Physical	Psychosocial	Cognitive	Behavioral
• Headaches	• Anxiety	• Decreased attention	• Over-medicate themselves and/or drink excessively
• Grinding teeth	• Irritability	• Narrowing perception	
• Clenched jaws	• Sadness		• Overeating or loss of appetite
• Chest pain, pounding heart	• Defensiveness	• Forgetfulness	
	• Anger	• Less effective thinking	• Impatience
• High blood pressure	• Mood swings	• Less problem solving	• Quickness to argue
	• Hypersensitivity		• Procrastination
• Muscle aches	• Apathy	• Reduced ability to learn	• Increased smoking
• Shortness of breath	• Depression		
	• Slowed thinking	• Easily distracted	• Withdrawal from others
• Indigestion	• Racing thoughts		
• Constipation or diarrhea	• Feelings of helplessness		• Neglect of responsibility
	• Hopelessness		• Poor job performance
• Increased perspiration	• Feeling trapped		
• Fatigue	• Lower motivation		• Poor personal hygiene
• Insomnia			• Change in religious practices
• Frequent illness			• Change in close family relationships

We resist change for three important reasons: not enough data or information, emotional fears, and lack of trust in the leadership. With resistance to change, the pace of implementation plans and productivity is impeded by acts of sabotage and non-compliance. People are caught up in their fears, regretting the past and what happened before—such as people being let go or relationships ending. Or they are worried and anxious about what the future will bring—a new manager, new team, new position, or new skills to learn.

The mind is stressing itself, vacillating between the past and the future. It is not in the present moment where creative solutions to problems can emerge.

Change stresses the ego. Our ego protects us and likes the status quo. It has a fear of failure because failure makes us look bad. For example it might say to you "I'm not a risk taker, I don't like new situations, I don't go first, I let others lead." The ego also holds us back from taking on new challenges. Fear, uncertainty, and doubt are excuses for not trying to rise above difficult situations. If we fail, our ego can blame other people and circumstances for not succeeding. With these attitudes adapting to change will be more stressful and challenging. [23]

We need to be self-aware to recognize when the ego is creating problems for us in dysfunctional ways that may be limiting our performance and causing us more stress than the situation calls for. Knowing our personal values, our strengths and weakness is a good starting point for developing self-awareness. As a leader, your personal values and behaviors affect the organization's values and culture. Being aware of the impact of leadership values on the organizational values is a necessary first step in aligning the culture with the desired values and behaviors needed for high performance and transformation.

Cultural entropy caused by limiting values and misalignment between personal values and organizational culture are other reasons for stress and low productivity. If values are a source of life force energy leading to high performance, then a person who cannot live their personal values is unable to access the energy, motivation, and inspiration that come from their values.

Limiting values drain energy and reduce capability and a person's ability to contribute their full potential. They make work more difficult and people less productive as they think more about themselves than the welfare of others. Organizations become dysfunctional when leaders demonstrate limiting values and become consumed by competition, power struggles, internal politics, and empire building—adding more stress on the employees and the organizational system.

23 Beyond Change Management, Copyright 2010, Dean Anderson and Linda Ackerman Anderson

Examples of limiting values:

- **Bureaucracy**—Bureaucracy is a form of institutionalised control. Too much bureaucracy can block employee creativity and entrepreneurial spirit, and takes away accountability, responsibility, and trust.
- **Internal Competition**—No communication between different parts of the organization.
- **Cost Reduction**—Competing for the same funding creates internal competition
- **Hierarchy**—Position dictates the quality and degree of communication with all involved. Access to key decision makers is limited. Power and status become the focal points.
- **Control**—Empowerment to make decisions is blocked. Creativity and innovation are reduced. Voices and contributions are not heard.
- **Silo Mentality**—Internal groups are not able to coordinate and cooperate.

Bottom-Line Impact

The following facts are from the Mental Health Commission of Canada:

- In any given year, one in five people in Canada experiences mental health problems or illness, with a cost to the economy of well in excess of $50 billion.
- Mental health problems and conditions account for more than $6 billion in lost productivity costs due to absenteeism and presenteeism (defined by Investopedia as a loss of workplace productivity resulting from employee health problems and/or personal issues).
- Mental health problems and illnesses account for approximately 30% of the short- and long-term disability claims.
- In 2010, mental health conditions were responsible for 46% of all approved disability claims in the federal civil service, almost double the percentage of twenty years earlier.

The factors causing high levels of stress leading to burnout and low productivity have a direct impact on cultural entropy, employee engagement and retention.

Cultural entropy is defined as the amount of energy in an organization that is consumed by unproductive work. It is a measure of the friction and pent-up frustration that occurs when potentially limiting values show up in the workplace. This exists when there is inconsistency or misalignment between personal values with the organizational values, misalignment of processes and a lack of mission and vision alignment.

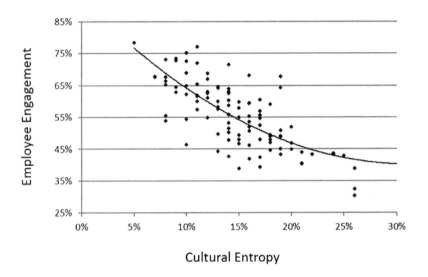

Figure 6-2—Cultural Entropy vs Employee Engagement

Figure 6-2 shows results from a paper written by the Barrett Values Centre. The research of 163 organizations demonstrated the relationship between employee engagement and cultural entropy. Note the strong inverse relationship between cultural entropy and employee engagement. Companies with high employee engagement have low cultural entropy. Companies with the opposite—high cultural entropy and disengaged employees—have leaders who are autocratic, greedy, and focused on meeting their own needs first. Companies with low cultural entropy and engaged employees have leaders who are collaborative, trustworthy, and build confidence and commitment with all their stakeholders.

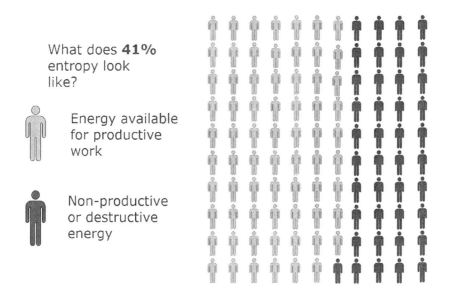

What does **41%** entropy look like?

Energy available for productive work

Non-productive or destructive energy

Figure 6-3 – % of Cultural Entropy – Productive vs Unproductive Energy

The organization in figure 6-3 has 41% entropy. This means out of 100 people coming into work, 41 of them (red) are not available or engaged to work. Their bodies have come in but their heart and minds have stayed on the bus or in the car park. How can an organization with this much entropy continue to be profitable and contribute in a meaningful way? It cannot.

In 2008, Iceland conducted a National Values Assessment. The results showed 54% entropy. Two weeks later the country announced bankruptcy.

Another example of the connection between sustainability, culture, and performance is ANZ Bank. In 1999, they were suffering from 49% employee engagement and faced the prospect of bankruptcy and the laying off of 150,000 employees. At this time they conducted a cultural values assessment to map, measure, and manage cultural transformation over the next five years. The results in figures x, y, z show the increase in performance as employee satisfaction increased.

Employee Satisfaction

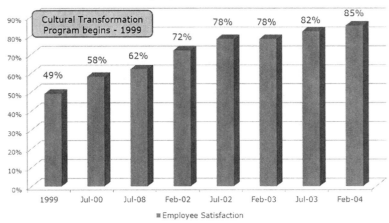

Figure 6-4 – ANZ Bank - Evolution of Employee Satisfaction

Net Profit after Tax ($m) - 11 Years

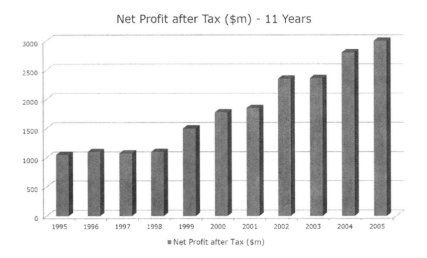

Figure 6-5 – ANZ Bank - Evolution of Profit

Figure 6-6 – ANZ Bank - Evolution of Share Price

These figures show a link between performance and culture. When leaders focus their attention and invest in transforming corporate culture to create a culture that is engaging and aligned with the personal values of their employees, profitability increases through increased employee satisfaction and performance. Healthy workplaces create happy employees who are less stressed, more focused and creative, and as a result more productive.

Transformational Leadership for Excellence
Transformation takes place inside and outside of individuals. Mental stress happens on the inside and has a debilitating effect on a person's performance. To facilitate internal transformation I recommend a program called TLEX (Transformational Leadership for Excellence). TLEX is a program that focuses on improving personal well-being by reducing stress, developing "soft" leadership skills, and strengthening team connectedness. It is based on the principle that leaders must first be able to lead themselves, before they can effectively lead others. The program provides tools and techniques that foster greater energy, clarity of mind, team cohesion and a passionate commitment to personal and team excellence. The ultimate aim of the TLEX program is transformation of the corporate culture, based on fostering of human values. www.tlexprogram.com

Worksheet 6-1 — Workplace Stress

Purpose: To explore the organizational stressors and how they affect employee performance.

What are some examples of 'stressors' in your workplace? Refer to table 6-1
On a scale of 1-5, how much support do you receive from your a.) colleagues? b.) supervisor?
How many hours on average do you work in a given week?

How are the above factors effecting your level of engagement and performance on the job?

What is one thing you can take personal responsibility for changing that will reduce stress and help you feel more engaged?

Part 3

Tools for Inner and Outer Transformation

The role of part three of the book is to give readers the tools to support inner and outer transformation. Change happens on the inside first, then manifests on the outside—like planting a seed and watching it blossom into its fullness.

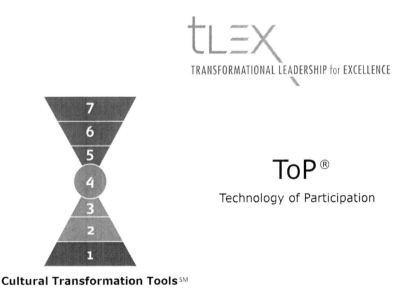

Chapter 7

Tools For Inner Transformation
The TLEX Program

Everybody is a leader. To lead people on the right path, our life has to be very pure... spotless.

It is every human beings birthright to live in a disease-free body and with a stress-free mind. Yet neither at school nor at home have we been taught how to deal with our negative emotions.

—**H. H. Sri Sri Ravi Shankar**

Self-Mastery for Inner Transformation

Transformation is a deeply personal experience. It is not the same as change or transition. It happens on the inside of a person when they perceive a new thought or evolve into something new. I am not the same person I was ten years ago. Over the past ten years I have taken many courses and programs in personal development. How I see the world now is quite different from how I saw the world ten years ago. The most significant changes have come in my personal relationships with my husband and children. With new awareness I see the world differently. Instead of blaming others, I'm curious and seek to understand what is happening in their world. I take responsibility for the things I can respond to. With this new mindset my relationships are healthier, more respectful, and more fulfilling.

As a corporate leadership consultant I have to be the first to experience a process before I can share, lead, and teach my clients a new method. This takes dedication to personal development and the desire to constantly learn, grow, and reflect.

There is a reason why the butterfly is used so often as a metaphor for transformation. The caterpillar emerges from the chrysalis having gone through several stages of transformation on its journey to becoming a thing of beauty so different from its origins. It is a journey of struggle and evolution, on the way to metamorphosis. The same is true for personal transformation. Every leader who embarks on the journey of organizational transformation must know that the journey begins first within them, because organizations do not transform—it is the people in them who do.

It is easy to blame others for the things that are not going well or are dysfunctional in your organization. As we point one finger in blame, there are three fingers pointing back at us. How are we responsible for what is happening? In most situations I have found we are part of the problem and part of the solution. The challenge is taking the time to reflect on the situation and gaining different perspectives on the problem so we can then develop the most effective solution.

What blocks or supports transformation is the state of our mind and quality of our awareness. Our mind is both the tool and object of change. When we encounter challenges or problems, do we respond or react? I used to react in difficult situations and in the process manage to alienate those I loved the most. My emotions would get the better of me and I knew I was not thinking clearly with all my mental abilities. Now, with more awareness, I respond with a curious mind that is more centered and calm.

Much of the personal awareness I have developed can be attributed to the tools and techniques taught on the TLEX Program. I'd like to share with you information about the program and recommend it as the first leadership development program for your leadership team. Why? Because before you can lead change, you must develop the skills to be able to access new sources of wisdom that will guide and empower you to lead transformational change. Otherwise you will continue to do as you have always done. And that is not transformation. Transformational leadership requires you to go inside and access new imaginal ideas through your intuition, awareness, and creativity.

Tools for inner transformation are those that develop inner awareness and access knowledge in our subconscious mind. To access wisdom at this level, one needs to still the thoughts of the conscious mind. This can be achieved through the breath and meditation. An added benefit to stilling our thoughts is the peace of mind, mental clarity, and rest it gives to the whole body. From the moment we wake until we go to sleep at night our minds are busy working at 14 to 32 cycles per second. This takes a lot of energy and is why we come home feeling exhausted even though we have not been physically active. Sitting for twenty minutes twice a day in meditation is a healthy practice for leaders to reduce stress, relax, and re-energize. The whole point is to do nothing.

Mounting medical research continues to suggest that our health, quality of life, and even the length of our life are all affected by our mental and emotional states. A piece of advice Eastern Yogis have given for thousands of years: take a deep breath and relax. Watch the tension melt from your muscles and all your niggling worries vanish. Somehow we all know intuitively that relaxation is good for us.

Now the hard science has caught up: a comprehensive scientific study has shown that deep relaxation changes our bodies on a genetic level. What researchers at Harvard Medical School[24] discovered is that in long-term practitioners of relaxation methods such as yoga and meditation, far more ''disease-fighting genes'' were active, compared to those who practiced no form of relaxation.

In particular, they found genes that protect from disorders such as pain, infertility, high blood pressure and even rheumatoid arthritis were switched on. The changes, say the researchers, were induced by what they call ''the relaxation effect,'' a phenomenon that could be just as powerful as any medical drug but without the side effects. ''We found a range of disease-fighting

24 http://news.harvard.edu/gazette/story/2012/11/meditations-positive-residual-effects/

genes were active in the relaxation practitioners that were not active in the control group," Dr. Herbert Benson, associate professor of medicine at Harvard Medical School, who led the research, says. The good news for the control group with the less-healthy genes is that the research didn't stop there.

More encouraging still, the benefits of the relaxation effect were found to increase with regular practice: the more people practiced relaxation methods such as deep breathing or meditation, the greater their chances of remaining free of arthritis and joint pain with stronger immunity, healthier hormone levels, and lower blood pressure. Dr. Benson believes the research is pivotal because it shows how a person's state of mind affects the body on a physical and genetic level.

But just how can relaxation have such wide-ranging and powerful effects? Research has described the negative effects of stress on the body. Linked to the release of the stress-hormones adrenalin and cortisol, stress raises the heart rate and blood pressure, weakens immunity, and lowers fertility. By contrast, the state of relaxation is linked to higher levels of feel-good chemicals such as serotonin and to the growth hormone that repairs cells and tissue. Indeed, studies show that relaxation has virtually the opposite effect, lowering heart rate, boosting immunity, and enabling the body to thrive.

What is the effect of stress on leadership? The qualities of a great leader have more to do with their personal attributes than their professional abilities. Qualities such as respect, honesty, loyalty, trust, and compassion are especially important for increasing employee engagement. They are also the qualities affected by the internal state of a person. If I am stressed and burned out, it means I have too much to do and not enough resources to do the work. Physically you might have headaches, grinding teeth, clenched jaws, high blood pressure, muscle aches, and shortness of breath. You may feel anxious, irritable, sad, angry, lethargic, or depressed. These feelings will have the effect of decreasing your attention span, narrowing your perception; you might become forgetful, less effective at thinking and problem solving. With these symptoms you might want to take medication just to get through the day. Or you may overeat, turn to alcohol and drugs to sooth your nerves, withdraw from people, procrastinate, and neglect job responsibilities. All of the above decrease your performance as a leader.

Executive Health in the Workplace

The following survey is an example of the ill-health that is affecting executive performance in organizations across North America and contributing to high levels of disengagement. The survey measured five elements of organizational health: work characteristics, social and interpersonal environment, stress, individual health outcomes, and organizational health outcomes. A total of 2,314 executives from across the federal Canadian Public Services responded to the survey, a 35% response rate that provides statistically valid results 99 times out of 100 with a margin of error of plus or minus 1.6 %.

APEX is the Association of Professional Executives of the Public Service of Canada. Since 1997 they have been conducting research on the health of federal executives and their workplaces. Survey results are contributing to a better understanding of the importance of a healthy workplace at both the individual and organizational levels. The work environment has an impact not only on the health of individuals but on organizational performance. The following synopsis paints a picture of the current reality of executive work, individual, and organization health in 2012.

Table 7-1 — Synopsis of APEX Health Survey Results

Work Characteristics
• 25% reported working more than 55 hours per week
o Working more than 55 hours per week has been shown to significantly increase risk of cardiovascular diseases and depression
• 59% of executives reported the use of technology increased their productivity, but
• 84% say that technology adds to their workload
• 46% indicate that technology contributes to a decrease in their work/life balance
• 3.8 on a scale of 7 indicated access to resources is below what executives need to accomplish tasks
o Trying to "do more with less" creates additional workload burden, which increases stress
• Imbalance between level of effort and reward
o 60% of executives felt that costs outweighed gains

Social and Interpersonal Environment

- Social support from colleagues—2.8 on a scale of 4
- Social support from supervisor—3.0 on a scale of 4
  - o Social support is at an all-time low
  - o Social support has been shown to be an effective buffer against adversity and stress. It is one of the most important protectors against burnout and distress.
  - o The absence of support from the supervisor is a significant risk factor for illness and absenteeism
- Interpersonal conflict—2 on a scale of 5
- Intergroup conflict—2.01 on a scale of 5
- Intragroup conflict—2.33 on a scale of 5
  - o Interpersonal conflict is a significant predictor of work environments perceived to be disrespectful
- Fairness at executive level—3.8 out of 5
  - o Unfairness can have a negative impact on commitment and engagement, and lead to burnout
- 22% of executives report being verbally harassed
- 10% say their workplace is disrespectful
  - o Top disrespectful behaviors include: not sharing credit, breaking promises, showing anger, blaming, telling lies, and making negative comments
- 39% of the source of verbal harassment is the direct supervisor
  - o Direct supervisors are the main source of disrespectful behavior in the workplace
  - o Harassment and lack of civility are measures of the type of workplace interactions that are having an increasingly harmful effect on individual and organizational health outcomes

Psychological Stress

• Executives are more stressed than 75% of Canadian adults
  o If sustained at high levels without respite, stress may lead to reduced immune response and result in medical conditions and illness
• 51% of executives report most days are extremely or quite stressful
  o The more days people experience as stressful, the more likely their performance and productivity will be affected

Individual Health Outcome

• 58% of executives report their physical health is excellent or very good
• 13% report their health is fair or poor
• 11% report mental health conditions – almost double since 2007
• A third of executives are experiencing sleep deprivation
  o People who do not get enough sleep increase their health risks, and their cognitive capabilities for decision making are impaired
• 61%—almost two-thirds of executives are overweight or obese
  o This puts them at risk for cardiovascular disease or type 2 diabetes
• Half of executives are sedentary
  o Rates of physical activity are insufficient to provide executives with the protective health benefits of exercise

Psychological Health

• 20% of executives use medications to treat depression, anxiety, or insomnia
• 46% of executives are reporting high levels of overall distress
  o Distress impairs day-to-day functioning and the ability to carry out normal tasks
• 21% of executives use professional counselling to deal with work-related stress issues
  o These issues are not only affecting their performance at work but are having an impact on their personal and family lives
• Individual resilience—12.2 out of 16
  o The most resilient executives are over 55 and the least, under 45

Organizational Health Outcomes

- Overall levels of commitment have dropped to 52%
  - o Commitment is recognized as an indicator or willingness to extend effort in order to further organizational goals
- Engagement levels have fallen
  - o 25% highly engaged
  - o 43% moderately engaged
  - o 32% actively disengaged
    - ◊ Engagement is an indicator of connection with work activities and ability to deal well with job demands. Engaged employees are more productive and better performing
- The public service ratio of engaged to disengaged executives is 2.1 to 1
  - o This ratio is higher than in the average organization
- 25% report symptom of severe burnout
  - o Symptoms include: emotional exhaustion, cynicism, and reduced sense of accomplishment
  - o Burnout arises as a result of highly motivated individuals striving to meet performance goals without sufficient resources and structures that would permit them to succeed
- 5.4 sick days per year
  - o Many executives are using vacation days for stress leave

Conclusions of APEX Health Survey

The causes of poor organizational health are rooted in the workplace. The same factors that are increasing the health risk to individuals are also causing greater risk to organizational health. In the APEX example, effort-reward imbalance, lack of respect, harassment, and low access to resources can contribute to poor mental health and increased risk for cardiovascular disease.

A sense of connectedness and support from colleagues and supervisors, being able to use one's skills, higher job control, perceived fairness, respect, and recognition would help to reduce the health risks. Addressing these factors will result in significantly improved executive health and well-being and have a considerable impact on the productivity and organizational outcomes. This is the value the TLEX program delivers.

What happens to your workforce when its leaders feel overworked, underpaid, harassed, disrespected, stressed, burned-out, not valued for their skills, and not supported by their colleagues and supervisors? You have an unhealthy, disengaged, unproductive organization that is wasting its human capital. How can an organization continue to be viable when 32% of its leaders are actively disengaged? Imagine the affect this has on the workforce.

How much do you think it would be worth to an organization if it invested in programs designed to reduce stress and increase relaxation, giving leaders the energy and clarity of mind to solve problems in a respectful, collaborative, and trustworthy manner? Wouldn't your performance improve if you were given the tools to reduce stress and create a workplace environment that had more integrity, fairness, and compassion?

Imagine how it would feel to be able to create a vision of the future with your people. An inspiring vision that a team has co-created is the glue that holds them together. Participation aligns team members around shared values and a common cause to make a difference. Creating common cause gives people the courage to endure the pain of change. Passion and positivity allow people to see past the negative obstacles to the bigger picture. Inspiration energizes people to work collaboratively and creates motivation and a positive attitude that can have a healthy rippling effect on the whole organization.

A New Leadership Paradigm

The TLEX program is a well-rounded approach to personal excellence and transformation, offered by the International Associations of Human Values (IAHV). The TLEX program seeks to provide a developmental framework for current and future leaders to be effective in the areas of:

- Personal empowerment and self-mastery
- Connectedness and trust—building harmonious relationships and team coherence
- Vision and inspiration—creating shared meaning and purpose

EXCELLENCE

Vision
&
Inspiration

③

Connectedness & Trust
Forging relationship and coalitions,
building trust

②

Self-Mastery & Energy

Calm and stress-free mind, healthy body

①

Figure 7-1—Three Tier Model of Change: Personal, Social, Organizational

IAHV is committed to fostering human values and social responsibility across all sectors of society, and in particular, with the TLEX Program in the corporate sector. It seeks to build personal excellence, creativity, enthusiasm, and overall happiness in the workplace. IAHV promotes the ability to have a stress-free mind and inhibition-free intellect, enabling individuals to achieve their full potential. The TLEX approach has proven effective for many of the world's leading private and public sector organizations such as: Accenture, Coca–Cola, Dell, GE HealthCare, the Government of Canada, Google, Harvard School of Business, IBM, IKEA, MIT Sloan University, Shell, The World Bank, and The World Health Organization.

Transformation happens when a person realizes they have a need for it and takes responsibility for change. In order to recognize the change required, one needs to have a calm and clear state of mind. Without a calm and centered mind, how can we think clearly and make the best decisions? When we are stressed our perception is clouded and we are not able to observe all there is to see. With clearer perception, what we are able to observe improves. Greater perception and observation leads to improved communication and creates the mental conditions for imagination, intuition, and creativity.

Scientific Research and Benefits of TLEX Program

Studies on the TLEX Program and its core practices have been conducted throughout the world. The specific techniques in the TLEX Program have been the subject of medical research and scientific study since 1995, and research on these practices has been published in international peer review journals.

Research at a premier institute for the study of neuroscience and mental health – the National Institute of Mental Health and Neurosciences – found a significant decrease in levels of cortisol (known as the "stress hormone") within 21 days of program participants learning the practices.

Independent research has shown that use of the tools and tangible techniques that are taught in the TLEX program significantly:

Reduce levels of stress (reduced cortisol, the "stress" hormone)
Relieve anxiety and depression (mild, moderate, and severe)
Strengthen the immune system
Enhance mental focus, clarity, and calmness
Enhance health and well-being
Increase awareness of self and others

Commonly reported results include:

- Increase in personal resilience and adaptability
- Increased level of responsiveness
- Increased level of energy and dynamism
- Tangible and direct impact on self and team
- Increase in team cohesion
- Positive impact on productivity
- Increased fulfillment at work
- Greater ease and joy in relationships
- A deeper sense of community

For a list of client references visit: www.tlexprogram.com

Case Study — The TLEX Program
Compensation Branch, Public Works & Government Services Canada (PWGSC)

The Compensation Branch at PWGSC is undergoing a multi-year change initiative, modernizing its forty-year-old pay and pension systems for the Government of Canada and streamlining its operations. Over a period of three years, from 2011 to 2013, PWGSC's Director General invested in five TLEX programs to better equip willing employees who were dealing with a stressful work environment with many difficult deadlines and interdependencies. The opportunity was open to all staff regardless of level; all that was required was a willingness to participate and be open to new ideas, as it was made clear that this would not be the typical classroom knowledge training that most were accustomed to.

The PWGSC TLEX Programs focused on three aspects of transformational leadership for excellence:

- Self-Mastery & Well-Being
- Leadership Skills—Communication and Trust
- Team Connectedness

Self-Mastery & Well-Being
Prior to taking the program employees reported that they were experiencing anxiety panic attacks, an inability to sleep, depression, and for some, the "super woman" syndrome (the need to do it all)—all of which were reducing mental clarity and work/life balance, contributing to health problems affecting performance and productivity.

After taking the course employees became aware of how important it was to make time and take care of one's self. When you are feeling better, and energized, with a positive mental attitude, you have a positive impact on those around you. If you are not well, it is hard to care for the needs of others.

Employees say that the breathing techniques they learned are still being used whenever they are faced with stressful situations on the job, at home, and before going to sleep at night. These techniques are enabling more clarity and mental focus, which is helping staff to make better decisions, to feel more in control and to be aware of themselves and others.

Employees who participated in the program gained practical ways to relax, de-stress, and deal with difficult situations at work and at home. The breathing techniques have been said to have reduced anxiety levels, enabling staff to let go of stress and diffuse panic attacks by returning them to the present moment. One person reported her last panic attack was before the course.

Participants say that the techniques have also helped calm those around them. Leaders and staff have become more sensitive and aware of others' needs. The breathing techniques and "slowing down" have improved mental clarity, posture, and awareness.

Leadership Skills—Communication and Trust

Before taking the program, in their fast-paced work environment with constant deadlines and pressure to perform, managers might ignore the opinions of others to accomplish tasks faster. They might leave others out of decision making unintentionally, assuming they already knew all the answers. This caused staff to resent decisions that were made without them. Managers had a lot of opinions that they thought they needed to share, but were not always listening to others. Individuals felt intimidated by people who were smarter than them. Perception of others was confused by what they thought they knew about them.

After the program, staff indicated that they felt less stress, a greater sense of well-being, and a much improved sense of perception. Individuals could see more potential in themselves and others. Their self-esteem and self-confidence appear to have increased, and in reducing the "super woman" syndrome of feeling the need to do everything, life has become more balanced.

The perception of the leadership role and its importance has shifted and changed. Ideas are now presented to the group and managers more often seek staff input and participation. This approach has created an inclusive team spirit among some of the teams, as members feel their opinions matter. Staff are happier that decisions are being made with their input. People reflect more before they share ideas, thinking first about others' needs and giving more room for others' opinions. With greater listening skills, managers are realizing how much they talk and they are actively listening to and hearing others.

To lead others, leaders first need to lead themselves. One of the program participants developed a greater sense of self-awareness about who they are, what they want in life, and where they want to go. They also learned what others thought about them, and how important it is not to be what others might perceive them to be. They developed greater self-mastery and self-awareness, learning more about their strengths and weaknesses, and gaining a comfort level for what they can do well.

Team Connectedness

Before taking the program some employees worked "as islands" in their workstations. They didn't know or make time getting to know each other. The offices were closed to others.

Through heart-to-heart conversations participants learned much about each other. They learned how others perceived them and had the opportunity to see the true personality and individuality of the people they were working with; who they truly are, what is important to them, and why they exist. Now they have a much greater appreciation for each other and realize their co-workers do exist! They have put aside pre-conceived ideas and appreciate knowing the individuals they work with.

The program has transformed the group dynamics among those participants. The staff developed a much stronger sense of acceptance and connectedness. The opinions, values, and experiences of team members are now more likely to be treated with respect that comes from knowing each other's strengths and weaknesses. Synergy and collaboration have developed from a better understanding of the interdependencies between teams. Staff can see where managers are coming from; together they are likely to smile and talk more.

All participants learned how important it is to:

• Be a good team leader
• Care that staff are having a hard time
• Realise staff are humans with feelings
• Be more humble

The teambuilding exercises taught the importance of the leadership role in holding a team together.

What Participants Found Surprising About the Course:

Participants were surprised to discover the potential they can bring to the job, how much they personally have to give to others, and how other people perceive them. After the initial awkwardness of sharing on a deep level, they found it helpful to feel the support and togetherness the team gave to each other, both emotionally and physically. Learning how effective the breath is at bringing them back to the here and now—the present moment—in times of distress or anxiety was useful. Participants discovered how easy it is to integrate the breathing techniques into real life whenever needed.

Value and Benefit of the Course:

It was a huge benefit getting to know co-workers on a deeper level. There is more respect, awareness, and value for team members as individuals—their strengths, weaknesses and contributions. This new awareness has strengthened work relationships, increasing trust. Having a better awareness of team members and what they are good at, enables managers to plan workloads more effectively.

Participant Comments after the TLEX Program, January 2013:

- "Who would ever have thought that the Government of Canada was this interested in the emotional and physical well-being of its employees? This course would have been unthinkable just 10 years ago. Bravo PWGSC, you've got your finger on the pulse. "
- "The information presented and learned on this course is beneficial across all aspects of life. I will apply the techniques at work and at home. The course is well delivered and helps to focus one on the self. Breathing is essential to all, yet so easily forgotten about."
- "What a wonderful surprise this course has been interweaving breathing, meditation and yoga to many people who would not otherwise seek out these activities is brilliant! Bravo!"
- "Everyone should have this course. It will make a big change in the work place!"
- "Encourage Managers to practice techniques that will help them understand their staff. Soft skills are not as present in Managers and I think it would result in a healthy working environment."

- "Happily surprised and glad to have been part of this course. I was very happy that we had the chance to be able to share experiences that we would not normally do during work hours. The closeness that I feel I have developed with my colleagues is very precious."

Increase in
Energy Levels
94%

Relaxation and
Reduction in Stress
89%

INDIVIDUAL

Improved
Clarity of Mind
91%

BENEFITS'

Changed
Paradigms About
Leadership
83%

ORGANIZATIONAL

Helped
Organization's Growth
and Improved
Work Performance
91%

Greater Sense of
Team Connectedness
93%

Figure 7-2—TLEX Survey of More than Thirty Companies

TLEX participant feedback gathered from 30 companies that participated in the program closely matches the comments gathered in the PWGSC case study. On a personal level, participants say they are more relaxed, and are using the tools and techniques to reduce stress. There is a greater sense of work-life balance and energy levels have increased. The techniques have helped improve mental focus and clarity by bringing the mind back to the present moment in times of stress, and focusing on the task at hand.

When there is a greater sense of well-being and stress is reduced, a leader's perception improves and they are more aware of their own potential and the strengths of their team. Self-esteem and self-confidence increase, and there is greater balance in life. Leaders are more aware of how to inspire and motivate others and help them believe in themselves. Managers develop emotional intelligence and learn how to grow and leverage it in others. Leaders who are aware of what brings joy to themselves and others are more empathetic and caring. These values are the basis for building trust relationships and strong teams, the foundation for organizational performance and growth.

Follow-up after taking the course is desired by staff to keep the team connectedness alive and explore ways to integrate the new insights gained into daily life. Leaders, managers, and staff learn new ways of being, and interacting with one another. Providing bi-weekly opportunities to share experiences keeps the organization learning and developing together, which helps in creating shared goals and values to build a culture of high performance. *To find out more about this program and how it can help support your organizational development visit:* www.tlexprogram.com

International Association for Human Values

The International Association for Human Values (IAHV) is a worldwide humanitarian and educational organization. It seeks to promote human values of empathy, commitment, dynamism, enthusiasm, and responsibility through workshops in personal excellence, transformational leadership, and service projects related to youth-led development, women's empowerment, disaster and trauma relief. *Visit www.iahv.org for more information on its mission and programs.*

One who is not amazed by the magnificence of this Creation, his eyes are not yet opened. Once your eyes are open, they close and this is called meditation.

Tell me, what in this Creation is not a mystery? Birth is a mystery; death is a mystery. If both birth and death are mysterious, then life is certainly a greater mystery. Isn't it?

Being completely immersed in the mystery of life and this creation is samadhi. Your knowing or believing doesn't really matter to what is. This Creation is an unfathomable secret, and its mysteries only deepen. Getting steeped in mystery is devotion. The "Scene" is a mystery; the "Seer" is a mystery.

Deepening the mystery of creation is science. Deepening the mystery of the self is spirituality. They are the two sides of the same coin. If neither science nor spirituality can create wonder and devotion in you, then you are in deep slumber.

—**H. H. Sri Sri Ravi Shankar**,
Founder of IAHV and the TLEX Program

Worksheet 7-1 — Personal Development and Self Mastery

Purpose: To develop greater self-awareness and self-mastery when things are going well and when there is stress

When things are working well

What is happening when you have a really good day at work? Who are you with? What are you doing?
How are you feeling?
What makes this a good day? Describe in your own words how people would recognize you are having a good day at work:
What do you need from other people to support you in having a good day at work?

Worksheet 7-2 — Personal Stress Points

What work situations cause you to feel stressed? What is usually happening in these situations?
Describe the feelings you experience in such situations. What *thoughts* do you have when you are experiencing stress?
Identify the *fears* that lie behind the thoughts that are causing your stress or anxiety?
What *needs* do you have that are not being met when you feel stressed?

Chapter 8

Cultural Transformation Tools

The Human Energy Field

When our personal and cultural energy fields are in alignment we live in a state of internal stability and external equilibrium. If it is out of alignment we need to change ourselves or our environment.

—Richard Barrett

Linking Performance to Culture

Building a values-driven organization is a key competitive advantage for the twenty-first century. The most successful organizations are consciously paying attention to and investing wisely in their organizational culture. To remain ahead of the game, leaders are attracting, engaging and retaining the top talent, who are motivated by leaders who create an inspiring vision of the future that give direction for the whole organization to follow. Leaders respond strategically to the changing economic conditions around them, ensuring continuous improvement and sustainable growth. How well they are doing all this by engaging employees and external stakeholders plays a big part in their success.

Today more than ever before in our history, people want to be engaged and have their voices and ideas heard. There has been a shift in values and mindsets. We have raised our children in an environment of asking their opinion and giving them responsibility for the choices they make. Now our children are coming into the workforce with the expectation of contributing to the decision-making process. Gone are the days when children were seen and not heard. Now they want to be seen and heard. With the experience of making decisions and being accountable for their choices, they expect to be consulted on issues that affect them.

The benefit to leaders is the access they now have to the knowledge our youth bring with them into the workplace. Our youth have been trained to brainstorm and work collaboratively in teams. They live and breathe connectivity with social media. This brings to life creative and innovative ideas. Their strengths are our weaknesses. Having a diversity of strengths to call upon creates high performing teams.

The link between performance and culture can be found in teams with a high level of trust. People want to trust and be trusted. In the *Speed of Trust,* Stephen Covey's formula for results is:

Formula for Results: Strategy x Execution x Trust = Results

Trust is a value that is found in high performing organizational culture. It is developed by leaders who influence and gain the trust of their employees. A leader's consistent behavior based on values of integrity, respect, and openness will build their credibility inside the organization and create a strong reputation externally with stakeholders in the community.

People want to work for ethical organizations that are making a difference and doing the right thing for society. Seeing leaders making the right choices for the right reasons, aligned with ethical values, sets the example for employees to do the same. In an environment with a high degree of trust and democracy—where employees are encouraged to contribute and voice ideas—employees will take responsibility and ownership for identifying problems and raising issues to management without fear of retribution. This reduces the cost of resolving problems and speeds the process of continuous improvement.

With democracy come the values of freedom, equality, fairness, openness, and transparency. Gone are the days of command and control where leaders led by fear. In the twenty-first century leaders are recognizing the power of change by the people, for the people. By creating workplace cultures that invite people to share the best they have to offer and enabling their full potential to show up, leaders are accessing a powerful life force in values that fuels high performance.

How do leaders create a values-driven organization and tap into the potential that values have to fuel high performance? The Barrett Values Centre Cultural Values Assessment (CVA) is a Cultural Transformation Tools^{SM} (CTT) that provides this capability. A values-driven organization takes decisions and actions consciously to create the future they want to achieve. Values fuel motivation and action. To create an inspiring vision it's important to know what values are motivating and driving people in the organization. The CVA provides this information by mapping and measuring the values of the organization, both the positive values that are organizational strengths and the limiting values that are causing entropy and reducing performance.

The CVA results show which values define the organization at its core. In today's business marketplace who you are and how you operate are just as important as the products you produce. Your values are a key differentiator in the internal culture of your organization and your brand—the external reputation you have in the marketplace. It's a competitive world out there. Knowing who you are and how you operate is critical information for leaders to influence, manage and lead by. Values-based leaders are empowered to build a better future for employees, customers and communities.

To succeed in the twenty-first century, values must be in evidence in every decision you make and every action you take. Leaders must "walk the talk" and operate with integrity. This practice makes the organization more resilient and adaptable to change. Guided by values, decision making is swift and congruent. An example of this took place during the 2008 outbreak of and deaths from listeriosis, linked to cold cuts from a Maple Leaf Foods plant in Toronto, Ontario. Within twenty minutes of calling a board meeting, the president decided to hold a news conference and take responsibility for the outbreak. As described in chapter four, the company's immediate actions resulted in the public continuing to trust the quality and safety of Maple Leaf products.

Along with direction and resilience, values create goodwill. In the above example, because consumers trusted Maple Leaf, they continued to believe in Maple Leaf's reputation of producing healthy, safe food.

Leading with values gives purpose and direction to decisions. In difficult times people want to know where the organization is going and what is driving its leaders. Clear values and a sense of purpose give people a sense of connectedness to the vision and where it is leading them: a solidarity around the shared vision and common values that support a collective goodwill. Leaders need to create this shared vision and unite people around values they all connect with. Human values have the power to unite diverse values and beliefs. Who doesn't want to be treated with respect, loyalty, and trust?

Values are the basis for meaningful relationships. Everyone wants to feel they can trust the people they are working with, whether the relationship is with a fellow co-worker or an external partner. Trust is at the foundation of all relationships. Without it the relationship will not survive.

How effectively an organization is able to compete is based on the levels of trust people have inside and outside the organization. With high levels of trust, people work together more effectively. Leaders who are authentic and behave with integrity are seen as more trustworthy. When there is a lack of trust there is usually cultural entropy. Entropy can be seen when people are operating out of fear-based beliefs. Beliefs such as not having enough will drive behavior of greed; not being loved enough will drive behaviors of manipulation and blame; not being good enough will drive behavior of competition.

Trust is a key factor for success. How well we trust our co-workers, managers and leaders will determine our level of engagement and directly affect the level of our performance. Leaders who put personal gain ahead of building the long-term future of the organization lose the trust of employees, customers, and the community. Leaders build trust when they are in touch with their values and live them authentically; when they show they care, others will care what they know.

Leaders and organizations also need to become trusted members of society. Recognized as such, they will gain competitive advantage over competitors, build resilience, keep top talent, and protect their investments.

Failure to live by acceptable rules can damage the bottom line and contribute to a company's failure. Poor moral judgment has been the downfall of major corporations like Enron, Tyco International, and WorldCom. It is no longer what you do that sets you apart but how you do it. This creates sustainable, long-term success.

Values don't just define your competitive advantage; they define your leadership style. Who you are and what you stand for are just as important as the quality of the product you produce. Leaders who do not pay attention to the values of the organization are a liability. They need to display the highest level of ethics and ensure employees do the same. Leaders are key influencers and must model the desired values that guide and give direction to the organization.

The current global climate, fast pace of change, and the rise in terrorism, addictions, disease, and stress are all affecting how we see the world and are making life more complex. The world we were raised in—the world that formed our values and beliefs—is no longer the world in which we live. This calls for a new leadership paradigm and way of making decisions. It is no longer prudent to make decisions based on past assumptions and beliefs—the way forward is to consciously make decisions based on values for the future we want to create.

The shift in human consciousness that is now taking place resonates with being the best *for* the world not just *in* the world. This happens when leaders put the interests of the whole organization ahead of their own. These leaders have an expanded sense of self-interest and they focus in on the larger goal of building a great organization. They identify with and care for the interests and concerns of every employee and stakeholder. In doing so, their consciousness expands. When consciousness expands, new possibilities and opportunities emerge, leading to new solutions and strategies that are good for all.

The values of the whole organization, its stakeholders, and the community in which it operates must be embraced, not just those of the leader. It is the act of participation and engagement in the selection of values that supports inner and outer transformation and strengthens commitment to a new way of being. Without such participation and alignment, employees and stakeholders will feel removed from the change; they may be unable to effectively embrace the desired values to support your strategic initiatives. When the values of all stakeholders are heard and considered, this fulfills the transformation values of being heard and feeling part of a decision-making process. This inclusion generates internal cohesion and supports the process of developing shared values.

Seven Levels of Consciousness Model

Spiritual	Service	(7)
	Making a Difference	(6)
	Internal Cohesion	(5)
Mental	Transformation	(4)
Emotional	Self-Esteem	(3)
	Relationship	(2)
Physical	Survival	(1)

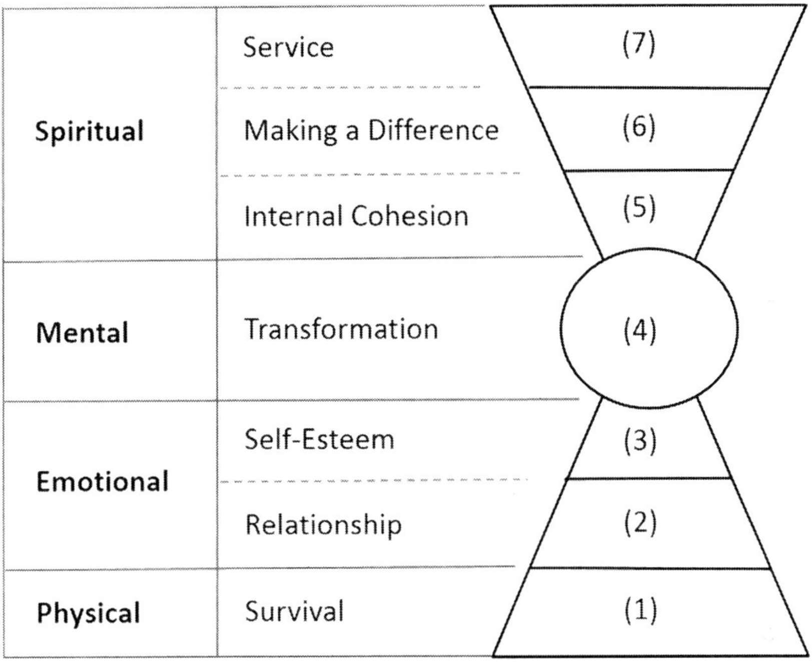

Figure 8-1—The Barrett Seven Levels of Consciousness Model

Origins of the Model

The seven levels of consciousness model provides a framework for mapping and measuring the values and behaviors that define an organization's culture. The model was inspired by Abraham Maslow's hierarchy of needs. In the model, hierarchy of needs is transposed into levels of consciousness.

The levels of consciousness relate to the basic human needs that drive our behavior. The first three levels of consciousness—survival, relationship, and self-esteem—relate to physical and emotional needs. These needs show up in behaviors that lead to causes of entropy in an organizational setting. Fears at the survival level, such as not having enough money, no matter how much they make, will drive behaviors of greed and control. Fears at the relationship level are about feeling they do not belong or are not accepted enough, which drive behaviors of wanting to be liked and dependence on others. Fears about performance and not being good enough will drive behaviors to seek status, authority, and competition.

At the fourth level of consciousness, transformation, we begin to seek who we truly are, freeing ourselves of fears and beliefs from the first three levels. At the fourth level, we want to make our own choices and develop our own voice; hence the power of facilitative leadership and its ability at this level to meet people who are ready to have their voices heard and contribute to decisions that affect them.

The fifth, sixth, and seventh levels are Maslow's level of self-actualization. The model expands into three levels to give more definition to our spiritual needs. At the fifth level a person wants to identify and live their purpose in life. They want to feel a sense of internal cohesion and lead a values-driven life. The sixth level is about making a difference. A person wants to collaborate with others who share similar values, mission, and vision. The seventh level is about service, where a person finds fulfillment in a life of selfless service. They operate with humility and compassion.

The seven levels of consciousness correspond to the needs that motivate and drive our behavior. If we are unable to meet a particular need our consciousness will remain at that level until the need is met. When it is met, our consciousness moves to the next level of development.

Defining Organizational Levels of Consciousness
The levels of consciousness are a practical way of defining and mapping our human values and behaviors. Another way of defining consciousness is *awareness with purpose*—the things we find important in life and on which we focus our attention.

Organizations grow and develop as individuals do, by mastering needs at different levels of consciousness. The goal of organizational development is to achieve full spectrum consciousness where actions and needs are being fulfilled at all the levels. The organizations that are able to master tasks at each level are the most conscious and have the greatest ability to adapt to today's challenges in the marketplace and the world.

Table 8-1– Personal and Organizational Levels of Consciousness

Level of Consciousness	Personal Actions and Needs	Organizational Actions and Needs	Developmental Tasks
7. Service	*Giving selfless service:* Being your purpose, compassion, humility, forgiveness, caring for humanity and the planet.	*Creating long-term sustainable future* for the organization by caring for humanity and preserving the earth's life support systems.	*Serving:* Safeguarding the well-being of the planet and society for future generations.
6. Making a Difference	*Making a positive difference in the world:* Reflecting empathy, alliances, intuition, mentoring, a focus on well-being.	*Building the resilience* of the organization by cooperating with other organizations and the local communities in which the organization operates.	*Collaborating:* Aligning with other like-minded organizations and communities for mutual benefit and support.

5. Internal Cohesion	*Finding meaning in existence:* Finding your purpose, integrity, honesty, authenticity, passion, enthusiasm, creativity, humor and fun.	*Enhancing the capacity* of the organization for collective action by aligning employee motivations around a shared set of values and an inspiring vision.	*Connecting:* Creating an internal cohesive, high-trust culture that enables the organization to fulfil its purpose.
4. Transformation	*Letting go of fears:* Finding courage to grow and develop, adaptability, continuous renewal, personal growth.	*Increasing innovation* by giving employees a voice in decision making and making them accountable for their futures and the overall success of the organization.	*Facilitating:* Empowering employees to participate in decision making by giving them freedom and autonomy
3. Self-Esteem	*Feeling a sense of self-worth:* Showing confidence, competence, self-reliance. *Fear-* I am not good enough, *Leads to* – need for power, authority	*Establishing structures, policies and procedures* and processes that create order, support the performance of the organization and enhance employee pride.	*Performing:* Building high-performance systems and processes that focus on the efficient running of the organization.

2. Relationship	*Feeling protected and loved:* Family, friendship, loyalty, respect *Fear* – I am not loved enough *Leads to* – Jealousy, blame	*Resolving conflicts and building harmonious relationships* that create a sense of loyalty among employees and strong connection to customers.	*Harmonizing:* Creating a sense of belonging and mutual respect among employees and caring for customers.
1. Survival	*Satisfying physiological and survival needs:* Health, security, financial stability *Fear* - I do not have enough *Leads to* – control, domination and caution	*Creating financial stability*, profitability and caring for the health and safety of all employees.	*Surviving:* Becoming financially viable and independent.

Mastering Organizational Needs

Each level of consciousness has developmental tasks for an organization to master.

The first three levels of organizational consciousness focus on financial security and profitability, relationships and customer satisfaction, and high performance systems and processes. Organizations with high levels of cultural entropy tend to focus on the first three levels and do not empower their employees. Enthusiasm and engagement is low because the organizations are run by authoritarian, controlling leaders who create a culture of fear and do not value participation. Employees in this type of culture feel stifled, unable to bring their full selves to work, resulting in high levels of disengagement and stress.

The fourth level focuses on adaptability, continuous renewal, teamwork, collaboration, and transformation. There is a shift from a controlling, fear-based leadership style, to one that is facilitative. Leaders encourage open, inclusive dialogue. Employees are engaged and empowered to share ideas and collaborate. They are given the freedom and responsibility to make decisions, be creative, and innovate. This kind of environment supports employees' personal and professional development, encouraging them to explore their strengths and let go of their fears.

Levels five, six, and seven are focused on cohesion, building mutually beneficial partnerships for the well-being of society. Organizations that concentrate on these levels without taking care of levels one, two, and three, will not be operating effectively and efficiently. They lack the skills to manage the finances, provide customer satisfaction, and implement systems to run the business.

Everyone views the world around them according to the values, beliefs and behaviors that are most important to them and define who they are. Organizations are the same. The values and behaviors that are most important to the leaders will define the organization's level of consciousness and create their culture.

The seven levels of consciousness model provides a framework for mapping and measuring an organization's culture. In diagnosing and assessing the organization's cultural performance, it provides a roadmap for developing implementation strategies that support change.

Cultural Values Assessments

One of the major challenges in transforming organizational culture has always been how to make the intangible tangible. In the late 90s, The Barrett's Values Center developed the Cultural Transformation Tools^{SM} (CTT), an innovative set of assessments that map the consciousness and values of individuals and organizations. In the past fourteen years over 3,000 value assessments have been conducted worldwide.

The CTT values assessment is a detailed diagnostic report of an organizational culture and a roadmap for continuous improvement. The tools are based on the seven levels of consciousness model: they allow the organization to measure the alignment of the personal values of the leaders and employees with those of the current culture of the organization, and those of the current culture with the desired culture.

A Proven Success
In 2000, a noted Australian Bank used the CTT assessment to understand its current values and to begin a program of cultural transformation. Between 1999 and 2004, the level of employee satisfaction rose from 49% to 85%. The shift in values was accompanied by a significant improvement in shareholder value and profitability.

> When I reflect on what makes an outstanding organization, what keeps coming back is the effectiveness of our people individually and collectively. Our responsibility as leaders therefore is to enhance, harness, and direct the capacity and energy of our people toward virtuous and valuable ends. Long term success has to have a solid foundation built on principles and values that act as a centre of gravity. In business, you get what you target, design, measure, provide incentives for, and are passionate about. This applies equally to principles and values, which need to be nurtured and directed through an effective whole-systems approach and values management framework.
> —**John McFarlane**, Chief Executive Officer,
> ANZ Bank, Melbourne Australia

The Leadership Team Small Group Assessment
One of the powerful tools offered, the Barrett Values Centre Small Group Assessment (SGA) for leadership teams, is important for two reasons: the senior group must i) be aware of the scope and depth of the cultural issues, and ii) be willing to take action, including commitment to personal change, before the rest of the company is involved in the process of cultural transformation.

Here are some key facts about leadership and stakeholder value:

- Leadership development drives cultural capital
- Cultural capital drives employee fulfillment
- Employee fulfillment drives client satisfaction
- Client satisfaction drives stakeholder value

Cultural alignment can occur at any level of consciousness, however, full-spectrum consciousness creates sustainable high performance and long-term resilience. Achieving full-spectrum organizational consciousness requires full-spectrum leaders.

The process of whole system change begins with the personal commitment of the leader and the leadership team to their own personal transformation. Why is this necessary? The culture of the organization is a reflection of the leaderships' consciousness. If you want to transform the culture of an organization, either the leaders must transform, or the leaders change. Organizational transformation begins with the personal transformation of the leaders. Organizations don't transform, people do!

A leadership team Small Group Values Assessment begins with a survey of the leadership group. The questions focus on positive leadership qualities and highlight the issues leaders need to address to achieve their potential and to grow as leaders. The CEO or the leader of the organization must be willing to commit to his or her own personal transformation in order to change the culture. *The leaders must be the change they want to see.*

After the leader and the leadership team have committed to the process with the Small Group Values Assessment, a Cultural Values Assessment (CVA) of the whole organizations can be conducted. The CVA delivers a scorecard of the organization's individual, current, and desired performance with which to measure the progress of cultural transformation over time.

Barrett Values Centre Cultural Values Assessment Benefits
- The CVA provides a way of managing the cultural evolution of the organization to the same level of detail that finances are managed.
- CVA results can generate deep, meaningful conversations about the purpose and strategy of the organization and the well-being of all stakeholders.
- The CVA provides a road map for achieving high performance, full-spectrum resilience and long-term sustainability.

Key Attributes of the Cultural Values Assessment
- **Short Survey** - The survey instrument asks only three questions, is available online and requires only fifteen to twenty minutes to complete.

- **Customizable** - The survey may be customized to the specific cultural and demographic needs of the groups being surveyed.
- **Demographics** - The richness of the CVA survey data is determined by the depth of demographic categories selected. There is no limit to the number of group categories chosen.
- **Cost Effective** - The CVA is affordable for both small and large organizations. Costs are based on the number and type of reports requested, not on the number of survey participants. Reduced fees are available in developing countries and for primary and secondary educational institutions.
- **Multiple Languages** - The survey is currently available in multiple languages or written dialects. Additional languages can easily be added.
- **Fast Turnaround** - A CVA typically goes from survey initiation to reporting in two to four weeks.
- **Alleviate Survey Fatigue** - The CVA assessment can be easily linked to the front or back end of other organization-wide staff surveys.
- **Option** - You can also choose to carry out an Espoused Values Analysis (EVA) for your organization or any demographic grouping. This analysis measures the degree to which the espoused values are being lived in your organization.

Barrett Values Center Leadership Values Assessment (LVA)

Leaders only grow and develop when they get regular feedback. Do you know what others appreciate about you? Do you know what advice your boss, peers, and subordinates can offer you to improve your leadership style? Do you know how you are contributing to the cultural entropy of the organization? Do you know your level of personal entropy? The answers to all these questions are provided by the Leadership Values Assessment.

The LVA is a powerful coaching tool for promoting self- awareness, personal transformation, and an understanding of the actions a leader needs to take to realize his or her full potential. The LVA compares a leader's perception of his or her operating style with the perception of their superiors, peers and subordinates. Emphasis is placed on a leader's strengths, areas for improvement, and opportunities for growth. The LVA reveals the extent to which a leader's behaviors help or hinder the performance of the organization, and to what extent fear influences decision-making. The LVA also measures the personal entropy and authenticity of a leader. Demographic categories, such as boss, peer, and team member, may be added to an assessment in order to view responses by the relationship to the leader.

Benefits
- The LVA deepens your understanding of what you need to do to become an authentic, " leader.
- The LVA measures personal entropy and how you are contributing to the cultural entropy of the organization.

Key Attributes
- **Expert Analysis** - The LVA provides expert analysis of your leadership style and what you can to do to improve your performance as a leader.
- **Customizable** - The LVA values template may be customized to reflect the cultural attributes of your organization.
- **Fast Turnaround** - The LVA report can be delivered to you within one week of the completion of the online assessment.
- **Multiple Languages** - The online survey and plots are available in multiple languages. Written reports are produced only in English. Additional languages can easily be added.

The list of Barrett Values Centre Cultural Transformation Tools[SM] **for mapping the values of organizations**

The following tables provide a list of the survey instruments that are available for mapping the values of organizational cultures from an employee and stakeholder perspective. More detailed information and sample reports can be accessed by going to http://www.valuescentre.com/products__services/

Table 8-2 – List of Barrett Values Centre Cultural Transformation Tools[SM]

Name of instrument	Purpose
CVA – Cultural Values Assessment	Used to create a comprehensive diagnostic of the culture of an organization or group of people with a shared purpose. Contains value plots and full written analysis. Measures values alignment, mission alignment and degree of cultural entropy.

CDR – Cultural Data Report	Same as CVA without the written report.
SGA – Small Group Assessment	Cost-effective way of mapping values of a group of fifteen people or less. Same as CVA without written report.
SOA – Small Organization Assessment	A cost-effective way of mapping the values of an organization whose entire staff consist of twenty-five people or less. Same as CVA without written report.
Merger / Compatibility Assessment	Uses CVAs of different groups to highlight cultural differences and support cultural integration. Also used for cultural due diligence.
EVA - Espoused Values Analysis	Provides a quantifiable measure of the degree to which employees feel aligned with the core values of an organization
CER – Cultural Evolution Report	Uses successive CVAs to analyze the detailed changes that have taken place in the time period between two Cultural Values Assessments.
LVA – Leadership Values Assessment	Used to provide detailed insights into how the leader's values/behaviors support or hinder the performance of his or her organization, department or team. Measures the level of personal entropy and the degree to which the leader's perception of his or her operating style aligns with the perception of his or her superiors, peers and subordinates. Outlines the leader's strengths, and areas for development.
LDR – Leadership Development Report	A more automated version of the LVA. Instead of providing free-form responses, the LDR asks assessors to rate the leader against a prescribed set of twenty-six behaviors that research has shown to be significant. The LDR is a cost-effective way of carrying out a large number of leadership feedback assessments.

IVA – Individual Value Assessment	Used to assess the degree to which an individual is aligned with the culture of his or her organization. Same assessment instrument that is used in the CVA.
PVA – Personal Values Assessment	A simple, no fee, online survey with exercises to give people a deeper understanding of their values. www.CultureLeadershipGroup.com/pva

Achieving high performance takes conscious leadership that will guide the organization in the right direction. The Cultural Transformation Tools provide the means to assess the culture and hear from all the stakeholders about what really matters to them. The data equips the organization to have meaningful conversations that shift the dialogue from "me" (self-interest) to "we" (what's good for all). With it, debriefing workshops open the door to understanding the strengths of the organizations and what is causing frustration and limiting people's potential. With the compelling reasons for change identified, energy, and enthusiasm will build. Together the organization creates a shared vision with shared values.

All of the above are critical for developing "engagement" communication strategies that create alignment and support for the desired transformation. The positive, life force values are identified along with the values causing entropy and energy drain. Leaders gain a clearer picture of their own personal mastery and develop greater awareness of others. Making the time for discussion and self-discovery, focusing attention on alignment between team and organizational values and the mission and vision of the organization, creates a sense of belongingness and commitment for collective action that will achieve high performance.

Case Study – Departmental Cultural Transformation

In 2010, Public Works and Government Services Canada (PWGSC) was dealing with complex, unprecedented change that was stretching systems and people beyond anything they had ever experienced. The Government of Canada was in a period of tough fiscal restraint—with a deficit reduction of $4 billion, 5 to 10% of departmental budgets were being cut, increasing the pressure on staff to do more with less. Retirements were seriously reducing the number of staff while there were changing demographics to serve, and new technologies were raising service expectations at a time when their client service was already considered too slow.

Daniel Leclair, Director General Service Integration Sector, was asked to form a senior leadership committee to deliver on the Client Service Strategy. Cultural transformation to change the values and behaviors of the leaders and staff was seen as a key driver to support the strategic initiatives.

The directors-general who would be instrumental in transforming the client service culture throughout the department were chosen from across the organization to join the committee. With client service reported at a 50% satisfaction rating in previous years for some of the business lines, senior leadership recognized that how they were doing business needed to change significantly. The change would entail a transformation from rigid accountability to stewardship (having control of $14 billion in government spending) balanced by speed and agility.

A leadership problem emerged within a year of starting the project. Discussion around the boardroom table was missing key voices. Those of the senior leaders who had been appointed to the Client Service Strategy committee were deafening in their silence. Their voices were silent because they were not attending the committee meetings.

Something was wrong, but what? Engagement and commitment should have been high. This initiative was very strategic and had the deputy minister's and assistant deputy minister's attention. Yet the seats were empty. In their place, the directors-general were sending their directors, who were sending their managers to replace them. Yes, something was definitely amiss.

It was time to diagnose the reasons for the malaise affecting committee members. It was time to make the intangible tangible and assess the committee's performance by mapping and measuring its culture. The stakes were too high for the strategic initiative to fail. This initiative needed the hearts and minds of the top leaders fully engaged or only a small measure of success would be possible.

The leader of the committee hired a Barrett Values Centre Cultural Transformation Tools[SM] (CTT) Consultant to conduct a Small Group Cultural

Values Assessment with the thirteen directors-general (DGs) on the committee. The diagnosis was a misalignment of personal values with the values being experienced in the current culture of the committee.

Ethics, Excellence and Leadership were personal values for seven out of the thirteen DGs. The concern was these values were not showing up in the current culture—a sign of misalignment that needed looking into. These values had also been selected by the DGs as desired cultural values, which meant the DGs considered them important going forward to achieve their goals.

What was the problem? Why weren't these values showing up in the current culture? What was happening to prevent them? These questions and more were discussed during the team debrief session to understand the assessment data report and develop strategies to increase engagement and commitment.

Experience shows the biggest single success factor in building a high performance organization is a cohesive leadership team. This element was a major factor with the DGs' leadership team, who identified creating internal cohesion around a renewed vision as a desired value going forward. To increase engagement, the meetings needed passion and commitment.

After reviewing the assessment results, the committee members met to renew their vision and mission and selected key values and behaviors to support their strategies. One answer to their problem was discovered in the committee's terms of reference—the word leadership wasn't mentioned anywhere in the document. This was a clear sign to the group how much leadership was a life force value and driver that fuelled their performance.

From that moment on they became a leadership team and not a committee. Their mission was to create a partnership of leaders to enhance, innovate, and develop services and processes to become a client-centric organization. The vision: to be the center of expertise and provide leadership in Client Service Excellence. With this horizontal vision and key values of *integration, collaboration, efficiency, and whole of government approach*, the leaders began showing up more regularly to meetings that translated into more rapid progress.

Over the past three years PWGSC has been in transition to become a client-centered organization. The following strategies have provided tangible results in terms of improvements to service, client satisfaction, innovative new programs, and employee engagement.

Client Service Strategies—
New Systems and Processes to Support Cultural Transformation
The Client Service Strategy (CSS) is changing the way PWGSC does business by shifting away from the hands-on delivery of some of its services toward the strategic management of its business. The CSS has two major components: *Renewed Service Offerings* and *Enhanced Client Focus.*

The Renewed Service Offerings has three subcomponents:

- **Comprehensive Service Agreements**: Departmental Service Agreements (DSA) create a strategic partnership between PWGSC and the client organization by defining:
  o Mutually compatible purpose and component objectives and expected mutually beneficial outcomes;
  o The principles that guide the behavior of individuals of the department and its client to ensure a work environment that is conducive to effective service delivery;
  o The menu of services to be delivered along with any limitations;
  o The financial arrangements including the cost of the services provided;
  o The overview of the roles/responsibilities, the amendment and dispute resolution process; and
  o The measurement/reporting of service performance, client satisfaction, and risk management.

This is a more comprehensive, cooperative and standardized approach to the mutual governance of the service relationship.

- **Clear Service Standards** provide a clear and published commitment to achieve a measureable level of performance that the client can expect under normal circumstances for all services provided by PWGSC. Service Standards help clarify expectations for clients and employees, drive service improvement, and contribute to results-based management. They also reinforce PWGSC's accountability by making performance transparent, and increase the confidence of Canadians in government by demonstrating its commitment to service.

- **Innovative Service Offerings** includes a "one knock" approach to streamline access to departmental services. PWGSC is also leveraging the expertise of the private sector to deliver services and introduce self-serve models of service delivery. This approach generates efficiencies, avoids duplication, and results in more uniform service. These and other approaches are being used to evolve its service offerings to meet its clients' needs and strengthen its program delivery.

The Enhanced Client Focus has three subcomponents:

- **Integrated Client Engagement** is one of the cornerstones of sound client service. Working with the department's various business lines, PWGSC developed a robust new framework to foster a more consistent departmental approach to client engagement and business relationship management. Specific techniques include:
  o Embedding people, communication and values at the project level to improve the client service experience;
  o Improved governance at service agreement level using the comprehensive service agreements mentioned above;
  o Improved consultative methods at the project, DSA, and cross-jurisdictional levels.
- **Increased Client Satisfaction** is the department's new focus. The establishment of a client satisfaction assessment, measurement, and feedback system is used to enable managers to know how well the organization is performing from a client perspective and be able to deal with any issues interfering with more satisfied customers. It also helps to ensure the reward and reinforcement systems in the organization are operating to create the proper incentives that make people want to commit their energies to the cause of client service.
- **Client Service Culture** — PWGSC is committing to service excellence on the part of its employees and affirming its importance to the organization's identity as a whole. In other words, it is enshrining service excellence as a cultural and an essential element of the CSS. Other measures used to anchor client service in to the organization include:

o Use of core client service competencies in hiring client-focused employees;
o Incorporation of the client service competencies in performance assessments to provide the feedback necessary to adjust cultural dimensions in response to changing client requirements;
o Use of tailored client service training courses; and
o Employment of a monthly service excellence award.

Achievements
The CSS has been in place since the spring of 2010 and many achievements have been realized during these past four years:

a) Departmental Service Agreement—nineteen signed Departmental Service Agreements;
b) Standard and Performance Indicators—Published three editions of *"Our Services Standards and Results";*
c) Service Offerings—Launched the *"One Knock"* approach with a single point of contact for Small Departments and Agencies; inventoried PWGSC services; streamlined service channels and contact points; launched workplace 2.0; launched centralized Pay service; initiated Smart Procurement Initiative; launched rethinking the Translation Bureau;
d) Clients and Suppliers Engagement—Developed a departmental Client Engagement Framework; held four PWGSC annual conferences on client service; developed senior client service governance;
e) Client Satisfaction: Developed and launched the PWGSC Client Barometer;
f) Client Service Culture and Employee Engagement: PWGSC client service course and client service awards, client service competency, two annual Client Service Weeks, rolled out people management philosophy; Leadership development, Mentoring and Coaching circles for individuals and groups.

Leadership Experience Leading Cultural Transformation
At different times it has been exciting, scary, stimulating, and discouraging.

What has been surprising is the need for flexibility, the difficulty in recruiting team members who can think outside the box and are comfortable in a context where rules are not yet written. Also surprising is how often it is necessary to repeat the same thing in different ways to get people to understand.

What has been delightful is seeing cultural change taking root, moving from awareness, to understanding to action. Hearing clients state they are seeing an improvement in the client relationship with PWGSC. Seeing the breakdown of silos as organizations were brought together to develop the service agreements, and planning the integration of transformation initiatives.

Where they struggled the most was:

- Keeping the momentum alive;
- Dealing with change fatigue in a period of deficit reduction;
- Trying to make inter-branch committees work on horizontal issues that were not the leaders main responsibilities, the pull of vertical line functions and responsibilities against horizontal functional roles;

How has the leadership team's work added value to the transformation effort:

- The team has added value by building bridges between branches to develop more integrated solutions for clients (from e-procurement to e-payment)
- The team now has a better understanding of its clients strategic priorities

The key learnings over the past three years:

- The process of negotiating the Departmental Service Agreements was more important than the final result;
- The process brought together various parts of the organization and identified client issues before seeking senior-level signatures;
- There were lots of fears related to the establishment and publishing of service levels standards;
- These fears were addressed by co-developing standards together that both parties could live with.

- The need for quick wins to get traction, which they were able to achieve with the signing of agreements and publication of standards;
- The need for a mechanism to reach down to all staff and show how they will be directly affected;
- This was accomplished with the development of core client service competency training, hiring client-focused employees, performance assessments and feedback, and monthly service excellence awards.

What new directions or initiatives are in the planning phases?
In additions to building on the above, the following initiatives are being added:

- *Integrated transformation:* identification of synergies between key transformations is taking place, development of an integrated approach to PWGSC Service Transformation;
- *Branding/Positioning/Centers of Expertise*: launching an integrated marketing plan; modernization of web presence with less sites, cost reduction as a driver of change, continue to renew and adapt;
- *Structure and Cost:* Adopt a center of expertise approach, lead and influence government-wide initiatives, adopt a government-wide mandate for key internal services to reduce duplication (HR, Fin., Corporate, Industrial Security, etc.)

Conclusion
Conscious leadership is a key component to driving and supporting the system-wide change. When Daniel Leclair was asked to describe the conscious leadership qualities he felt were instrumental in supporting the PWGSC transformation, he identified the following transformational leadership competencies:

- **Diplomacy** – having the ability to bring together different points of view and strong personalities;
- **Engaging communication** and good listening skills;
- **Self-awareness** – recognizing the need and having the ability to change yourself as well as the organization; it's not just about producing results but engaging people in the vision and challenges;

- **Rational and emotional** – must work with the head and heart, the emotions of people, and being aware of the impact you have on their lives;
- **Inspire** staff with the benefits;
- **Empathize** with the challenges;
- **Co-develop** solutions that will make those impacted want to engage;
- **Access the wisdom** of the group to develop competencies together with managers;
- **Validate** with experts to bring credibility;
- **Energy to sustain the momentum and make it all happen.**

On the whole, the Client Services Strategy provides the means to fundamentally improve the nature and effectiveness of the PWGSC relationship with its clients on an ongoing basis. It provides the tools and techniques to ensure the relationship is managed and maintained from a strategic viewpoint with a commitment to closer cooperation. All together it enables a workplace culture that fosters teamwork, consistency, discipline, and the proactive sharing of information.

Worksheet 8-1 — Compelling Reasons for Change

"Never doubt that a small group of thoughtful committed people can change the world; indeed it's the only thing that ever has."
—Margaret J. Wheatley

Purpose: To build leadership team commitment for cultural transformation by conducting an environmental scan and identifying the compelling reasons for change.

Process:

- Bring together members of the leadership team for a group discussion.
- Divide team members into small groups of two or three, or remain as a large group, depending on the time available for the discussion.
- Hand out questions to different teams for small group discussions. Capture notes on flipchart sheets for presentation back in plenary.
- Plenary discussion to share findings.
- Develop common understanding of the business environment.
- Identify the compelling reasons for change.
- Allow two to three hours for this workshop.

Stakeholder analysis: Who are our stakeholders? What do they need from us? How do we serve them?

External business environment: What changes are affecting our organization and generating new business imperatives?

Internal business environment How do we constantly learn from our experiences and daily operations? How do team members bring themselves fully to work?

Organizational and social structures: How do we develop clarity on team objectives between all stakeholders? How does the team best organize itself to deliver on priorities?

The forces that hold the team together:
What is the level of trust on the team?
Using the Trust Matrix in Chapter 5 - Figure 5.3, plot five areas of strength and five areas that need developing.
What would motivate team members to give more to this team versus other teams?

Chapter 9

Conscious Leadership

What is the mind? Vibrating consciousness.
The organizational values of individuals have
energetic resonance to create the future.
Consciousness creates matter.

—Gita Bellin

Personal Alignment

My husband and I have been married for twenty-five years. Like many long term relationships we have had our ups and downs. During some of the challenging times, our different beliefs and values created conflict and a feeling of separation, driving a wedge in the love and connection we felt for each other. Particularly challenging conversations for us were about politics, where our opinions seem to be polar opposites. We'd end up in conflict, with raw emotions and hurt feelings because we could not agree with each other and there was no sense of togetherness on the topic. Have you ever had this feeling in a relationship close to you?

One day I was teaching a yoga class, feeling very grounded on my mat on the hardwood floor, calm and centered as I spoke. The theme for the day was "Skill in Action," how valuable it was to apply the skills you learn in life to all aspects of living. As I was teaching the lesson a realization began to dawn in me. Why not use all your training in human dynamics and communication to solve my own relationship problems. There was a chuckle inside my head as I heard myself laughing at how self-centered I'd been. It's one thing to teach the knowledge and another to really live it.

From that day forward I became more aware of the motivational values of people around me and what made them tick. I did a lot of soul searching on my own values. I discovered one of my top values is commitment. By living this value more authentically I recognized how much more satisfying it was to feel committed and live the value of commitment, than it was to focus on our differences. Our different beliefs were not going to change any time soon, and, quite possibly, they exist to spark growth in each other. However, what did change as a result of the shift in mindset and focus to accepting my husband's values and who he was, was a new outlook that has made our relationship happier and more joyful.

The more awareness and self-mastery you develop of your own values, the more consciousness you develop for appreciating and understanding the values of others. One way to do this is by observing yourself or asking someone about one of their values—why this value is important to them, what they do to live this value, and how they would feel if this value is stepped on or ignored. You will see their life force come alive: their demeanor shifts, their facial features lift and brighten, and their tone of voice has more energy and life.

This process has helped increase my capacity for conscious leadership and acceptance of people for who they are. When people feel accepted it strengthens the relationship: they feel your compassion and understanding. Leadership is more about these personal qualities than it is about accomplishing tasks. When you can touch and inspire the life force inside a person, you have found a key to higher performance.

My husband's views still have the power to challenge me when we talk about politics. The difference now is I do not pin negative feelings on him because we have different points of view. I think instead about the effect the conversation is having on my emotions and how different his values on the subject are from mine. I accept our differences rather than thinking to myself "he's wrong and I'm right." With the new mindset of acceptance I'm able to manage my feelings by observing the different perspectives and values at play. The feelings of conflict soon evaporate as they have nothing to hang on to.

Conscious leadership is an emerging concept in business and organizational development, where the requirements of leadership are expanding to meet the evolving consciousness of external stakeholders. Leaders are being asked to integrate values such as ethics, integrity and transparency, along with non-traditional business concepts such as co-creation, love, and wholeness in the management of profit, people and process. To ensure employee engagement, other concepts equally important to conscious leaders and conscious leadership are the encouragement of humor and having fun, showing employee appreciation, empowering human potential, and working toward common good (win/win) for all.

Imagine you had the good fortune to work for a conscious leader in a conscious organization. What would it be like?

Excerpt from *Conscious Capitalism: Liberating the Heroic Spirit of Business*, by John Mackey, Rajendra S. Sisodia, and Bill George. Harvard Business Press Books, 2013.

"The business is built on love and care, rather than stress and fear, whose team members are passionate and committed to their work. Their days race by in a blur of focused intensity, collaboration and camaraderie. Far from being depleted and burned out, they find themselves at the end of each day newly inspired and freshly committed to what brought them to the business in the first place—the opportunity to be part of something larger than themselves , to make a difference, to craft a purposeful life while earning a living.

Think of a business that cares profoundly about the well-being of its customers, seeing them not as consumers but as flesh-and-blood human beings whom it is privileged to serve. It would no more mislead, mistreat, or ignore its customers than any thoughtful person would exploit loved ones at home. Its team members experience the joy of service, or enriching the lives of others.

Envision a business that embraces outsiders as insiders, inviting suppliers into the family circle and treating them with the same love and care it showers on its customers and team members. Imagine a business that is a committed and caring citizen of every community it inhabits, elevating its civic life and contributing in multiple ways to its betterment. Imagine a business that views its competitors not as enemies to be crushed but as teachers to learn from and fellow travellers on a journey towards excellence. Visualize a business that genuinely cares about the planet and all the sentient beings that live on it, that celebrates the glories of nature, that thinks beyond carbon and neutrality to become a healing force that nurses the ecosphere back to sustained vitality.

Such businesses—suffused with higher purpose, leavened with authentic caring, influential and inspirational, egalitarian and committed excellence, trustworthy and transparent, admired and emulated, loved and respected—are not imaginary entities in some fictional utopia. They exist in the real world, by the dozens today but soon by the hundreds and thousands. Examples of such companies include: Whole Foods Market, The Container Store, Patagonia, Eaton, The Tata Group, Google, Panera Bread, Southwest Airlines, Bright Horizons, Starbucks, UPS, Costco, Wegmans, REI, Twitter, POSCO, and many others. In decades ahead, companies such as these will transform the world and lift humanity to new heights of emotional and spiritual well-being, physical vitality, and material abundance. Welcome to the heroic world of conscious capitalism."[25]

---

25   *Conscious Capitalism* – John Mackay, Raj Sisodia, 2013

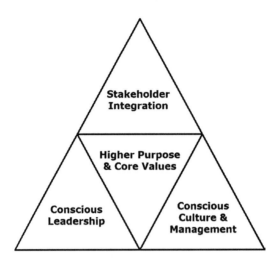

Figure 9-1—The Four Tenets of Conscious Capitalism

It is not possible to build a conscious business without conscious leadership: leaders who are passionate and motivated to create a vision for the organization that has a higher purpose to create value for all stakeholders; leaders who look for creative win-win, synergistic approaches to delivering multiple levels of value at the same time.

The old school of leadership from the corner office with a charismatic leader who knew it all, is evolving to a new style of "shared" leadership. Leadership is evolving as our consciousness in society is evolving. To keep up with the fast pace of change, the practice of shared leadership is also far more adaptable and resilient. The role of the leader today is to create an environment where collaboration and alliances are not only supported, but flourish. This is how the most successful, values-driven organizations are operating.

Leading yourself and leading others is not the same thing. You must be able to lead yourself before you can effectively lead others. Leading an organization is even more demanding and requires an additional set of competencies and skills.

Using the seven levels of consciousness model, leaders can work toward achieving full spectrum leadership consciousness and mastering the competencies at the different levels:

1. Survival consciousness by creating an environment of financial security and physical safety for themselves and those in their charge.

2. Relationship consciousness through learning to communicate openly, and by creating a culture of caring and belonging that engenders employee and customer loyalty.

3. Self-esteem consciousness by measuring and monitoring progress towards the organization's goals, and keeping the organization focused on quality, excellence, and continuous improvement, such that employees feel a sense of pride in the organization's performance, and can pursue their professional growth.

4. Transformation consciousness by becoming responsible and accountable for their actions, learning to delegate appropriately, empowering their executives and managers, and encouraging them to pursue their personal growth.

5. Internal cohesion consciousness by finding a personal sense of purpose/mission to their lives; creating a vision of the future that is a source of inspiration for everyone in the organization; and engendering a climate of trust.

6. External cohesion consciousness by actualizing their own sense of purpose through collaboration with external partners in strategic alliances and enabling their employees, managers, and executives to do the same.

7. Service consciousness by aligning the needs of the organization with the needs of humanity and the planet and performing acts of selfless service with humility and compassion that support their employees, managers and executives in doing the same.

How does conscious leadership affect cultural transformation?

With greater self-mastery and awareness, leaders create conscious environments where employees are empowered to co-create and collaborate with others to develop solutions in the best interest of the whole organization. The culture of a conscious business is a source of great strength and stability. Leaders operate with high integrity and transparency, and are flexible and passionate about learning how to improve.

This level of self-awareness, compassion and appreciation are developed in a leader from the inside out. It is also supported from the outside in by the conscious management systems and processes that run the organization.

Hence the importance of personal transformation programs like the TLEX Program to develop self-mastery. Leaders need to transform both internally and externally to become the change they want to see, "walk the talk" and model the transformation they are after. Those who do not align their personal behavior with the desired organizational values, create a path to failure: it breeds distrust, increases employee resistance, and damages building employee commitment for transformation.

Four-way alignment is needed to consciously lead whole system change within an organization. Refer to figure 9-2 below.

Personal Alignment of the leaders is the first of four quadrants that need to be aligned for successful transformation. This makes it possible for conscious leaders to approach change in all quadrants and all levels to produce maximum results and support whole system change.

Second is *Structural Alignment*. This is alignment between the espoused values that the organization has chosen and the behaviors that support and drive the structures, policies, procedures, and rewards of the organization. Like the leader, the organization must also "walk the talk."

Third is *Values Alignment*. This alignment is between the personal values of employees and the values they experience in the work environment. Employees need to feel they can bring their whole selves to work and do not have to park

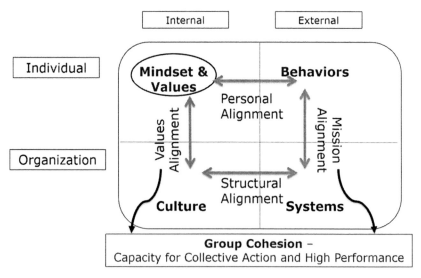

Figure 9-2—Four Way Alignment for High Performance

their best at the front door. There must be a sense of autonomy, equality, responsibility, fairness, openness, transparency, and trust.

Fourth is *Mission Alignment*. This is alignment between the employee's sense of purpose, role and responsibilities, and the purpose of the organization. Employees value the work they do, they are engaged and committed, understand how their work supports the vision and mission, and know where the organization is headed.

To successfully implement cultural transformation, change must be managed in all four quadrants at approximately the same time. It takes conscious leadership to personally align values and behaviors and effectively influence the values and behaviors of the collective. This is why change starts with the personal transformation of the leaders and a cohesive leadership team.

The Facilitative Leadership Way

Striving for 100% engagement

The Gallup Organization regularly surveys the workforce to measure levels of employee engagement. The latest figures for North America show that only 26 to 30% of the workforce consists of engaged employees (loyal and productive). Over half, 54%, are not engaged (just putting in time), while 16% are actively disengaged (unhappy and spreading their discontent). In Southeast Asia employee engagement is even lower, between 6 to 12%.

Why is such a high percentage of the workforce not engaged? Is it because old forms of security and certainty have disappeared and we haven't figured out how to operate standing on a bowl of Jell-O? Regardless, we all may be in need of new tools and processes to increase active engagement.

We are moving out of the information age and into the age of consciousness where people are relating to the world in a deeper, more meaningful way, caring for the world around them and their role in it. People appreciate that collective participation leads to better solutions and commitment to those solutions.

A town hall meeting that engages and mobilizes the community is not the same as a chat room or an email exchange. The communal results of thinking and taking action together to find new solutions are vastly different. The facilitative leadership approach is one that engages people, directly, not by technology proxy.

Facilitative leaders are engaged in:

- asking questions to enrich engagement
- sharing knowledge and information
- linking minds
- learning and unlearning

The Facilitative Leadership Way means shifting from "keeping control" to new ways of asking questions and relating to people so they can assume more responsibility. Helping a group face its challenges lets them build a clear picture of the situation then move on actions together. Facilitative leaders empower others without the use of power or authority.

A Transformation Wave

The use of a facilitative leadership style that helps people think and take action together is sweeping the workplace. Being a facilitative leader means working together to tie thinking and action to the organization's strategy, mission, vision and values, and the capacity for people to carry it out.

When working strategically, a group's thinking and planning stays connected to:

- The historic—what has happened in the past in the organization?
  - o   What was the original passion/plan?
- The present—what is going on now?
  - o   What is the current mission/message?
  - o   What are current accomplishments?
- The future—what is needed and what are the priorities for the future?

Use Leverage to Mobilize Strategic Action
Focus on Nine Points of Leverage

Using leverage mean placing the most emphasis and energy to get maximum strategic advantage from your actions.

Experience with client organizations has shown that certain dynamics in an organization provide more leverage than others. The nine points where leverage is most likely are shaded in the Dynamics Screen in figure 9-3. The leverage dynamics are numbered in order of importance.

The leverage point in the Economic Dynamic identifies client needs and drives everything in today's organization. The five leverage points in the Cultural Dynamic are: clarifying purpose, shaping the work environment, creating shared values, releasing team spirit and developing innovative methods. These dynamics are critical in creating an atmosphere of commitment, synchronizing time and space with the purpose and ensuring the importance of people as a guiding principle for the organization. In today's workplace, team spirit is essential. Finally, the three leverage points in the Political Dynamic are: ensuring information access, articulating clear expectations, and determining appropriate consensus.

Since the greatest emphasis during the last four decades has been in the Economic Dynamic, it is not surprising that the greatest leverage today is in the Cultural Dynamic in order to rebalance thinking in an organization.

You get the most results from your efforts when you:

1. Identify client needs to understand the demands of today's marketplace.
2. Clarify common purpose to understand who you are and why you are involved in the organization. When the purpose changes, all the other dynamics must be realigned with the new purpose.
3. Make certain there is meaningful information access so people can be involved and engaged—significant engagement. The key is learning how to quickly extract meaning from data and information.
4. Reshape the work environment and culture so the use of time, space and relationships support the common purpose.
5. Create shared values that highlight what is important in the operating values.

Table 9-1 — Changing Operating Values

From:	To:
"We have a job to do."	"Let's do what is needed."
"No one tells us anything."	"Who are we serving?"

"What are we doing?"	"What is our responsibility?"
"We can't try this."	"What would happen if?"

6. Release a team spirit that mobilizes energy and commitment with an entrepreneurial attitude.
7. Develop innovative methods to grow knowledge. Encourage and train people in leading facilitative conversations that solve problems, clarify issues, change work patterns, and create new ideas.
8. Articulate clear expectations to empower people to act like owners and get things done. Leadership models expectations consistently.
9. Provide support for appropriate consensus decision making.

Finding the places for greatest leverage and prioritizing becomes the guide for moving strategically when managing change.

When change turns into a struggle, look at these leverage points to find what is needed. First observe and measure what people care about, talk about and do. Then share information to deepen awareness and build self-confidence and empowerment. The key is to assess where to put emphasis to make the most impact with your efforts.

"No man is an island" in today's knowledge-based global society. We learn and grow in leaps and bounds when we get together and share our experiences. This is why facilitative leadership is a valuable competency for leadership, teams, and organizational performance. It is empowering for employees to be engaged in learning conversations that access the wisdom of the group and enable people to participate and contribute to the growth, development, and success of a company. When individuals feel a sense of empowerment they are living a life force that is unstoppable and will enable the organization to reach its goals.

How are you offering your people deeper meaning at work while at the same time achieving your organizational goals?

How do you connect and awaken the inner life force that inspires and drives employees to get up and face each day anew?

Most leaders have this desire, but are committed to a way of thinking that treats people as a means to an end. For organizations to prosper, each person needs to connect their sense of purpose to that of the organization's mission and

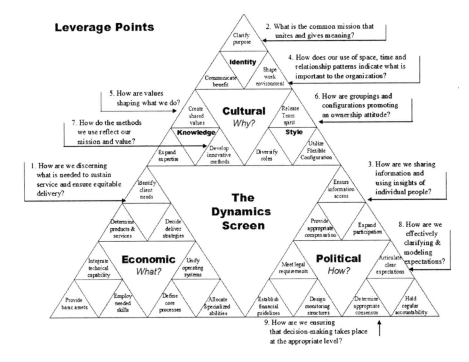

Figure 9-3—Nine Leverage Points for Strategic Action
Reference: Institute of Cultural Affairs, Social Process Triangles;
The Facilitative Way: Leadership That Makes A Difference

purpose. Understanding how to connect with people on a deeper level is the first step. Becoming a more proficient facilitative leader or manager helps in building a more meaningful, engaging, and empowering work environment.

Leaders who adopt a facilitative approach engage others in developing vision. Most visionary leaders are enriched when they interact with the ideas of others. Visioning together builds the kind of commitment that vision needs. Facilitative leadership has great potential for change.

When managers adopt a facilitative approach, they increase the possibility of building powerful teams that bring visions and plans into reality. Working directly with those who implement projects and plans increases their efficiency and effectiveness. Facilitative management builds strong organizations.

The Technology of Participation (ToP®) Group Facilitation Methods provide facilitation disciplines and roles that are necessary to support transformation and change. Equipped leaders engage their people by exploring topics in ways that surface different experiences and associations on a topic or issue. When combined, the insights form a new picture and create a new level of conscious awareness, generating new ideas or solutions to customer problems. Unleashed creativity and innovation can then be the genesis for new products.

Evolution of Consciousness

"The impact of development as economic growth is beginning to push against the boundaries and carrying capacity of the Earth and its biosphere. For this reason, we need to learn how to cooperate with each other for the good of the whole, and to do this we need an integral approach". [26]

The four-way model of alignment in figure 9-1 is an adaptation of the integral approach. It incorporates the whole-system approach to change and identifies the interconnections that affect each quadrant. Human systems such as teams within an organization, are interconnected and cannot help but affect other teams they come into contact with. When we apply the seven levels of consciousness model and results from a cultural values assessment to the whole-system approach to change, we can see how the desired values and behaviors will create collective action and group cohesion that lead to high performance. It takes conscious facilitative leadership to lead the evolution of an organization through the transformation process.

Each of us is evolving every day. In our personal lives and at work, we seek to fulfill our basic human needs. Every individual, team and organization is seeking to do the same. We spend our lives living to meet our internal needs in response to the experiences happening outside in our external world.

We start out seeking to survive and become productive, viable members of society. As we grow and develop, we join organizations to fulfill our purpose and feel a sense of self-worth. As we continue to grow, we bond with our colleagues and form teams. Eventually we learn the value of cooperating with others to create partnerships and strategic alliances that enable us to combine our strengths and achieve even greater goals. This mirrors the evolution in consciousness as we grow and develop from "me" to "we" to "us" on the journey to successfully fulfilling and mastering our growth needs in response to the world around us.

---

26   *Love, Fear and the Destiny of Nations, Volume 1, The Impact of the Evolution of Human Consciousness on World Affairs*, by Richard Barrett, 2012

Case Study – Municipal Government Challenges

Regional municipal leaders recently had a meeting with the theme of Building and Leading Exceptional Performance Culture. The leaders, who were interested in learning how to keep evolving and developing to build high performing workplaces, were invited to a facilitated workshop to discuss the current challenges facing their administrations. The insights that emerged pointed to challenges involved with the evolution of consciousness as we learn to master the seven levels of consciousness and apply the leadership skills needed to effectively meet the external drivers of change.

The following challenges were shared:

Level 1 - Talent management and leadership development are being put on the back burner during tough economic times, yet as the baby boomers retire, preparing new leaders is a priority.

Level 2 - Various kinds of engaging communications are needed to connect and respond with stakeholders.

Level 3- The old style of leaders who want to meet goals and objectives at all cost are having a tough time creating work environments that are fun and espouse work-life balance. As people retire or move to other organizations it is tough to attract and retain top talent.

Level 4 - Leaders struggle in finding the balance between different opinions of staff and board members. Intergenerational cultural differences between baby boomers and Gen Y make leadership a truly challenging job.

Level 5 - Leaders want to cooperate and build consensus to meet the hopes and expectations of their communities.

Level 6 - The pace and scope of managing complex change with multiple internal and external stakeholders is increasing very fast and driving organizational change.

Level 7- It's hard to deliver in a complex environment. Leaders want to manage and adapt to continuous change while serving the needs of society and a growing community.

These are but a few of the challenges facing the new style of conscious leadership. They demonstrate how the demands of our external environment are evolving faster than leaders within organizations are able to adapt to and keep pace with.

When we look at the old school of leadership and compare it with that of the new, we can see the evolution of conscious leadership emerge.

Table 9-2 – Evolution of Conscious Leadership

Old School of Management:	New School of Management:
• Senior Management had the answers • Control and efficiency drove advantage • Employee value was evident in "doing" • Shareholder dominant	• Those closest to the customer have the answers • Talent engagement and development drives advantage • Employee value is evident in "thinking" • Multiple important stakeholders
Old School Leadership:	**New School Leadership:**
• Moved up through the ranks to build know-how • Built "left-brain" dominant skills – strategy, financial • Saw what needed to be done and got everyone to do it • Mantra "make money for the shareholder"	• Must be comfortable with change • Need a balance between left-brain and right-brain skills (empathy, meaning, creativity, etc.) • Need strong relationships throughout the organization to stay connected to rapidly changing needs and employ "nobody is as smart as all of us" • Mantra "highly engage all relevant stakeholders"

Reference: Robert Seguin, The Productive Leadership Institute

The evolution of leadership consciousness can be seen through the development of business paradigms. Before mechanization we had the age of agriculture, with the ox and plough to till the fields. Many hands were involved in the process and leaders were the overseers. The amount of manpower you had determined your wealth and status, and this was enough to compete. Then came the industrial revolution with the introduction of mechanized tools and processes. If you were a little farmer doing things by hand, you soon realized that to compete, you needed to transform your agricultural processes and mechanize the tools and machinery to compete. The age of information introduced new tools again—the personal computer and the knowledge worker. Instead of being the "doer," employees became the thinkers. Information management and services became the processes replacing manufacturing as the driver of wealth creation.

With the dawn of the twenty-first century, we are entering a new business paradigm, the age of consciousness. Leaders are being required to change what and how they lead or face the consequences of being left behind. To get the most from their resources leaders must create new work environments to help knowledge workers maximize the volume of information at their fingers. The new competitive advantage is how effectively organizations collaborate and work together to develop new solutions for the growing needs and opportunities of solving society's global challenges.

Having one leader in charge of everything is no longer a leadership style that will enable an organization to compete and remain in business. With the fast pace of change, there needs to be leadership at all levels. People need to be resilient and ready to adapt minute by minute.

Work environments that can create a collaborative spirit with values that enthuse and energize the workforce, will provide employees with the resources to keep pace with increasing demands and workloads. Knowing the values and behaviors of your people that will drive high performance is a competitive advantage. Having a culture that attracts, engages and retains the best talent is another valuable strategy. This is the goal of building a high performing workplace—to awaken the life force in your values that will create a conscious culture of excellence.

Awaken your conscious leadership with cultural transformation coaching via an Individual Values Assessment at: www.CultureLeadershipGroup.com/iva

To access valuable bonus facilitation tools and techniques
become a member at: www.CultureLeadershipGroup.com

Worksheet 9-1 — Cultural Leverage Points

Purpose: To develop an understanding for the cultural dynamic leverage points within the organization.

Process:

- Bring together members of the leadership team for a group discussion.
- Divide team members into small groups of two or three, or remain as a large group, depending on the time available for the discussion.
- Hand out questions to different teams for small group discussions. Capture notes on flipchart sheets for presentation back in plenary.
- Plenary discussion to share findings.
- Develop common understanding of the business environment.
- Identify the compelling reasons for change.

Customer needs:
• How do we decide what our clients need?
• How do we ensure we are meeting and serving the needs of our clients?
Common purpose:
• What is the core business of the organization?
• What is the common mission that unites us and gives us meaning?

Employee engagement:
- How do we share information with our employees?
- How are we gathering and using the insights of our employees?

Work environment:
- How do we use space, time, and relationships to identify what is important to the organization?
- How are values shaping what we do?

Part 4

Dawning of a New Age

A new paradigm is emerging in the business world that is changing leadership consciousness—how they think and act about the health and performance of their organizations. We are moving from the information age, where knowledge capital was our key concern, to the Age of Consciousness, where cultural capital is driving transformation.

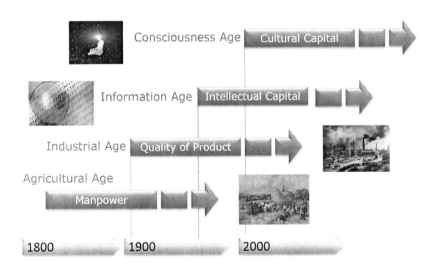

Figure Part 4 - Evolution of Business Paradigms

·

Chapter 10

21st Century Paradigm Shift

By 2020 the market leaders in all industries will be companies that have fully embraced the concept of conscious capitalism, including social responsibility and environmental stewardship. For business to be successful in the 21ˢᵗ century they will need to be more ethical, more enlightened and more focused on the common good.

—**John Mackay**, CEO Whole Foods

The Age of Consciousness

A new paradigm is emerging in the business world that is changing leadership consciousness—how they think and act about the health and performance of their organizations. We are moving from the information age, where knowledge capital was our key concern, to the Age of Consciousness, where cultural capital is driving transformation. Cultural capital is the value that can be placed on the way of being or "personality" of an organization.

No longer is it acceptable to ignore our responsibility to the environment and the responsibilities we have as corporate citizens to all our stakeholders. It has now been accepted that we, as a human race, are responsible for climate change and are destroying the planet with deforestation and mining, forcing species to extinction, emitting tons of carbon causing ocean acidification, depleting food, water and energy supplies. More than ever before, we are aware of the damages we are causing planet earth and there is a growing consciousness to do something about it. *The Age of Consciousness is dawning.*

Back in 2006, I was elated to see Ellen DeGeneres in an American Express commercial, meditating. Seeing a pop icon on national television meditating told me mindfulness had become mainstream. Seven years later, more people understand the meaning of the word consciousness and its implications than ever before. This is a result of an increasing number of people searching for meaning, purpose, and connection in their lives. We can thank thought leaders such as Depak Chopra[27], for his Quantum Physics, Neuroscience and thought leadership in connecting spirituality with science. The younger generation, those who have the most to lose, have had enough of the current ways of doing things, where greed is having devastating effects on the economy and planet.

There is no denying that our awareness has been evolving at a fast pace, probably due to the speed of change happening all around us. A few years ago the word "conscious" meant being awake and aware of what was going on around you in your immediate environment. Unconscious meant being asleep, knocked out, or unaware of what was going on around you.

In the new Age of Consciousness, "conscious" means something much more. It may be more akin to mindfulness, awareness of one's existence, thoughts, feelings and environment. And it goes even further—being awake, alive, accepting of life as it is, connecting with others on deeper levels, being

---

27 Depak Chopra, Indian physician,http://en.wikipedia.org/wiki/Deepak_Chopra - cite_note-Chopra_web_bio-1 holistic health/New Age guru and alternative medicine practitioner. Chopra has written more than 75 books, including 21 *New York Times* bestsellers. His books have been translated into 35 languages and sold more than 20 million copies worldwide.[11]

present to the bigger picture, and the greater good for all. It is the recognition of interconnection between ourselves and our world: the most profound level of responsibility imaginable, that each of us, and our thoughts, feelings, and intentions create the world we live in. Karl Jung meet Buddha. Eckhart Tolle high five.

What evidence is there for the Age of Consciousness?
The Age of Consciousness is gradually unfolding in all areas of society from our daily lives to our business practices. It seems that everywhere we turn there is reference to mindfulness or consciousness, people making a difference, changing our world, or giving back in some form or another. Conscious philosophies and practices are gradually finding their way into mainstream society. In time, this can only lead to a huge shift in humanity.

Only last week I was listening to the radio and there was a talk show on Conscious Dating. Being married for twenty-five years, I was curious how the single life is evolving. It appears, singles are now being told to listen to their intuition when they first meet a person to whom they are attracted. Don't wait for three dates to finally listen to the "little voice in the gut."

Artwork is becoming diverse and inclusive. Recently I was visiting the Head Office of an international bank and a beautiful painting caught my eye. Admiringly, I walked closer and noticed there was a Hindu God in the center of the painting. To the left was an image of the seven chakras. I expect to see paintings like this at retreat centers in exotic places, not in banks in the middle of Toronto, Canada.

Two weeks ago I heard a story about a café in the Toronto Beaches area with a quote from Eckhart Tolle on a bulletin board. When my friend told the chef she liked it, he told her of his passionate plans for developing consciousness in children around the world.

In the last three years, a government department has invested in five programs in Transformational Leadership for Excellence, designed to reduce stress, increase well-being, mindfulness, soft leadership skills, and team connectedness. Mindfulness appears to be moving into the public domain.

A few months ago an electrician arrived at a client's office with "Habitat for Humanity" written on his shirt. I asked him why and he told me it was a charity his company supports.

And these are just a few local examples—what about the Bangladeshi bank focused on ending world poverty, or the increasing cafés around the world that operate on donation only, or the vast number of businesses that donate to charities?

More people than ever before are talking about consciousness, mindfulness, and social change. It is not uncommon to have deep, connected conversations with strangers about the rising consciousness of people on the planet.

Widespread change is affecting the way we view and operate in the world. We are operating in a different paradigm. Whole disciplines or fields are metamorphosing into more conscious practices.

The professions of facilitation and coaching are examples of new careers that have developed over the last twenty years in response to our growing desire for self-awareness and continuous learning. Leaders have an increasing desire for awareness and consciousness to understand the world around them and how they can improve their skills through self-awareness and awareness of others. By asking questions, the facilitator/coach empowers us to go inside to find the answers. We are led to access our own internal wisdom, connecting with our intuition and sub-consciousness mind, making us more consciously competent.

Heart, Mind and Soul Connection

The heart is no longer just the organ that pumps blood through the body. It is no longer something that must be left at home with your emotions when you go to work, and it is no longer considered second to reason. Increasingly we are hearing about the influence of heart wisdom, a voice not to be ignored. Heart wisdom is now seen as vital to every aspect of our lives, from disease prevention to ensuring brand loyalty.

People are connecting more and more through heart-based dialogue, even in executive boardrooms. Vulnerability is now recognized as an important component in connecting with others. Only a few weeks ago I saw an email post by a CEO asking for feedback on the connection between vulnerability and the influence of leaders.

Research is mounting that mindfulness and conscious business practices can benefit each of us in all aspects of our lives. Corporations and law firms are bringing in the TLEX Program to teach their staff mindfulness and other meditation practices all around the world. What a shift!

It is not uncommon to see the words spirituality, mindfulness, and consciousness in mainstream venues and on mainstream programs in a variety of industries and domains.

No longer are yoga, meditation, mindfulness, and conscious practices just optional extras at "hippy" health retreats in beautiful remote areas around the world. They are now mainstream activities—not only popular outside of work, but also an important part of corporate well-being programs.

People are calling for mindful mediators and psychotherapists, and groups are forming that promote conscious business practices. Coaches, counselors and psychologists alike are recommending mindfulness and conscious-based practices for stress relief, increasing mental clarity, the management of depression and anxiety, and the treatment of some personality disorders, and so on. We have mindful eating practices to assist with weight loss and food enjoyment.

Conscious Business

Business has not been left out of the shift to the Age of Consciousness. The movement to conscious capitalism is happening around the world as some of the most successful companies such as Google, Amazon, and Pepsi shift away from traditional shareholder models to ecological models of business. Leaders view their corporations, organizations and businesses as an ecosystem with all parts equal to each other. Employees are as important as customers, who are just as important as the community, who are just as important as suppliers, who are just as important as shareholders and so on. Successful businesses are following these principles. Competitors who do not follow suit may find traditional business models unsustainable. Customers want to know businesses care and are contributing to society.

Conscious Law

It must be the final frontier when the legal system recognizes the need for the law to take the well-being of individuals and society into consideration. Judges and magistrates around the world are now taking well-being into account in their determinations. Get used to it—therapeutic jurisprudence is growing. Some lawyers in the U.S. are now seeing their role as healers rather than warriors. They are now considering not only legal rights, but mental, emotional, and physical health when advising their clients. Wow!

Restorative justice practitioners, contemplative lawyers and transformative mediators are incorporating new billing practices designed toward happiness. Contract drafters are helping their clients align plain language documents with the purpose and values in which they are interested. Collaborative lawyers are looking out for the well-being of their clients, finding things they have in common instead of the differences.

Times are changing and a gradual shift in humanity is taking place. In time, as the power shifts to those more consciously aware, the destructive patterns of human behavior will cease or minimize, and we will learn how to live consciously together in harmony.

Development of Cultural Capital

Financial capital is dependent on cultural capital, which is dependent on human capital. To understand how cultural capital came to be, it helps to understand the evolution of business paradigms up to the Age of Consciousness.

The Agricultural Age

The best documented shift in business paradigm is the Industrial Revolution of the 1830s. Before the Industrial Revolution, we lived in agricultural societies. During the Agricultural Age, labor consisted of manpower living off the land in rural areas. The more manpower you had, the more land you could farm, the more crops and surplus you could produce for trade.

The Industrial Age

The Industrial Revolution changed all this. Mechanization made it possible to change from hand-produced goods to industrially produced goods. The change in production methods from manual labor to machine-driven production systems included a significant shift in management practices and how people worked together. Mass production marked the beginning of the consumer society. Because of mass production, the produced goods were now available at more affordable prices to a larger public.

The Information Age

With the introduction of affordable personal computers and the Internet in the 1970s came the information age, an economy based on information computerization. During the information age, our knowledge-based societies created high-tech global economies. Transactional decision making significantly lowered costs for both the producers and buyers. With the ongoing adoption of new technology in daily life, education, and business, the information age has provided rapid global communications and networking to shape our way of life.

In the industrial age, many immigrants migrated to the New World. In many cases immigrants were industrial workers, with little or no schooling to speak of. First generation immigrants saw the potential and power equalizer in education. It was a parent's dream to provide the means for their children to get a good education and maybe even a university degree. In our lifetime, most of us have attained a high level of education, and have become knowledge workers. Intellectual capital has become our greatest value.

The Age of Consciousness

Since the onset of the new millennium people are becoming more conscious of the world in which we live and work. For leaders and organizations to remain competitive and high performing, they are realizing the need to expand their focus on quality, productivity, talent, and knowledge management to include their vision and values, what they stand for and how they work together to achieve their goals. Leaders are now more conscious and aware of the culture of the organization defined by how aligned people are, how well they cooperate, and how well they execute.

Developing cultural capital in the Age of Consciousness means making an investment in how people work together and the "personality" of the organization. Financial capital is dependent on cultural capital, which is dependent on human capital. Values drive cultural capital and inspire human capital. This means it is necessary to measure and manage the values of an organization and its leaders to ensure the health, performance, and capacity to remain competitive.

For companies to achieve sustainable excellence they must be healthy. This means they must manage both their performance and health. In a 2010 survey[28] companies undergoing transformation revealed that organizations focused on performance and health simultaneously were nearly twice as successful as those who focus on health alone, and nearly three times as successful as those who focus on performance alone.

The center of attention the last four decades on business renewal has been on performance improvement. Now, with the emergence of consciousness, leaders recognize they need to spend more time on improving the culture and the health of the organization because this is where the need is. When leaders were surveyed as to which area they wished they had more information, only 16% of leaders chose "determining what needs to be done to generate near-term performance." On the other hand, more than 65% of leaders chose "determining what needs to be done to strengthen the company's health for the longer term."

Organizational health is defined by internal alignment, quality of execution, and capacity for renewal. All of these factors are determined by organizational culture and depend on how effectively people work together. The following nine values drive cultural capital and inspire human capital for high performance and competitive advantage:

Shared vision: Having a clear sense of where the organization is headed and how it will get there, with direction that is meaningful to all employees.

Leadership: Leaders inspire action by others. There is personal alignment between the values of the leader and the espoused values of the organization. They walk the talk and lead by example.

Shared values: Everyone in the organization understands the organizational values and expected behaviors that provide quality interactions and a climate of respect, cooperation and trust.

Responsibility: Individuals take ownership and are given responsibility to make decisions and deliver results.

---

28 *Beyond Performance*, 2011, Scott Keller, Colin Price

Engagement and Commitment: Employees are empowered to share ideas, experience, and knowledge to evaluate organizational performance, and develop solutions to address issues and opportunities when they arise.

Capabilities: Skills and talents are developed to ensure employees are capable to execute the strategies which create competitive advantage.

Inspiration: The presence of enthusiasm that drives employees to put in extraordinary effort to deliver results.

Collaboration with External Partners: The quality of engagement with customers, suppliers and partners and other external stakeholders to drive value.

Continuous Learning and Innovation: Managers facilitate collaborative dialogue to ensure the quality and flow of new ideas and the organization's ability to adapt and shape itself as needed.

Financial capital is easier to measure and manage as a corporate resource than cultural capital. This is because organizations have spent the last century developing accounting systems to track finances. Cultural capital is more challenging because values and behaviors are intangible. However intangible it may be, it is still a very important corporate resource that needs measurement and management. What you measure you can manage and improve. Much like the organization's finances which are measured weekly and monthly, so too do the organization's culture, values, and behaviors need to be monitored regularly by managers and leaders.

How do we find symptoms of ill-health? In the mindsets and values that drive behaviors that obstruct management practices that lead to healthy culture. Bringing the mindsets and values to the surface and working with them consciously is the only way to make sustainable change happen. Missing this step will cause the transformation to be a failure. In the 2010 survey, none of the organizations that did not work on diagnosing mindsets and values rated their transformation as "extremely successful." Whereas, those organizations that did go beneath the surface to map and measure their values and behaviors, were four times more likely to rate their transformations "successful."

Conscious Leadership

The core requirement for developing cultural capital is the right kind of conscious leadership. Leaders need to combine resilience and emotional capacity to continuously improve themselves as they continuously improve their organization. They make the change story personal by offering compelling reasons for change and engaging others. They model the desired behaviors and values and by so doing, the capacity for personal transformation. Attention and investment are made at the top of the organization to create a leadership team whose members are aligned and trust each other. Leaders are the number one champion of the change efforts and are seen involving themselves personally in the change.

The Shift from "Me" to "We"

Before I built my house ten years ago I never expected to be sorting my garbage into five different containers: 1. recycling (paper, glass, and metal); 2. compost (good for the garden); 3. newspapers; 4. pop cans; and 5. the real deal. Back then I did not value the time and effort required to be environmentally conscious. When I moved into the newly constructed home in a community that took environmental protection seriously as a community value, I changed my mindset towards sorting garbage.

The value toward the environment changed to match my community's and with it my behavior changed. The reason behavior changed was I felt a sense of connection to the community's vision and sense of purpose. Now I take pride in sorting my garbage and saving all the compost possible. I have aligned my values to the common good of a cause greater than myself. I can honestly say there has been a shift in consciousness from "me" to "we" for the greater good of the community.

Recently I had a salad at a well-known fast food outlet. When I went to throw out my garbage I was shocked to find there was no recycling bin. Just to confirm, I asked the manager if the restaurant chain recycled their garbage and the answer was no. We still have a long way to go before corporate levels of consciousness catch up with individual levels of consciousness in society.

Corporate social responsibility is not the same as being a conscious business. Conscious business practices go deep in the fiber of the core values that guide the organization. They believe in creating value for both communities and the environment, whereas corporate social responsibility programs are seen as add-ons and dismissed as "green-washing."

Table 10-1 – Corporate Social Responsibility Versus Conscious Capitalism

How Corporate Social Responsibility Differs from Conscious Capitalism	
Corporate Social Responsibility	Conscious Capitalism
• Shareholders must sacrifice for society • Is independent of corporate purpose or culture • Adds an ethical burden to business goals • Reflects a mechanistic view of business • Is often grafted onto traditional business model, usually as a separate department or part of public relations • Sees limited overlap between business and society, and between business and the planet • Is easy to meet as a charitable gesture; often seen as "green-washing" • Assumes all good deeds are desirable • Implications for business performance are unclear • Is compatible with traditional leadership	• Integrates the interests of all stakeholders • Incorporates higher purpose and a caring culture • Reconciles caring and profitability through higher synergies • Views business as a complex, adaptive system • Places social responsibility at the core of the business through the higher purpose and viewing the community and environment as key stakeholders • Recognizes that business is a subset of society and that society is a subset of the planet • Requires genuine transformation through commitment to the four tenets • Requires that good deeds also advance the company's core purpose and create value for the whole system • Significantly outperforms traditional business model on financial and other criteria • Requires conscious leadership

To help individuals find organizations that share their values, there is a new transparency tool designed to make going green profitable. Why? Nearly half of all global consumers are willing to pay more for goods and services from companies that have implemented programs that give back.[29]

"Not only are consumers making purchase decisions with purpose top of mind, they are also buying and advocating for purposeful brands." says the 2012 Edelman goodpurpose® Study.

The study found 72% of consumers would recommend a brand that supports a good cause over one that doesn't—a 39% increase since 2008. Some 73% of consumers would switch brands if a different brand of similar quality supported a good cause—a 9% increase since 2009.

The more consumers lean towards giving money to companies that are truly doing good business and being more transparent, others will change, and we will see real, systemic change. Consumers have the power to influence the way the world does business. Change will happen when consumers demand that companies they buy from mix in a little green where the bottom line has always been about red or black. Change will happen when companies cannot afford not to.

Go to www.eco-profiles to show the world what you are doing environmentally.

The twenty-first century paradigm shift into the Age of Consciousness is bringing with it higher levels of consciousness. We are connecting with the world on a deeper level, being present to the bigger picture and greater good. It is the recognition and acceptance of our interdependence and sense of responsibility for the world around us—that every choice we make has an impact and that one person can make a difference. When a group of individuals share the same values and behave in the same way, collective action leads to change and greater outcomes.

Translated into organizational behavior, when individuals decide to act with good intentions for the common good of the larger group, the collective action of the whole organization, altogether living its values in the same way, will create a highly aligned and successful company.

The shift from "me" to "we" is a shift from personal self-interest to doing what is best for the common good of all. For many individuals a shift like this does not seem practical and brings with it buried fears and personal history. The fears might be connected to security (not having enough), relationships (not being loved enough), and self-esteem (not being good enough). An example of

29   The Nielsen Global Survey on Corporate Social Responsibility

this is a manager being asked to loan an employee to another team for a period of time to ensure the timely delivery of a product to a client. The loss of one employee will mean one manager will not achieve her goals. If fears were guiding her decision she might not let go of the employee because of the fear of not achieving her goals, and how this might be perceived by her team, colleagues, and management. However, with trust in her leadership team and living the core values of cooperation and collaboration, she knows her performance will not be penalized; instead her behavior will be recognized and rewarded.

Values-driven conscious leaders empower the organization to shift from "me" to "we," and create cultural capital that is good for all. They provide direction and a concrete inspiring vision of the future that gives everyone a common sense of meaning and purpose. They are transformational leaders who engage employees in dialogue, empowering them to voice ideas, experience, and knowledge. They create cooperative, collaborative relationships based on trust. Building commitment and with shared goals and values encourages people to work for a common cause. With respect and honesty, they model open communication and ensure staff have the necessary skills to achieve results.

When staff has the basic needs of security, relationships and self-esteem taken care of, the shift from "me" to "we" is a natural process of growth in personal development. Individuals find personal fulfillment from being engaged and the ability to contribute their knowledge and experience. Together Everyone Achieves More spells TEAM. Through cooperative collaboration and continuous learning, individuals are performing higher and as a result the whole team and organization performs better. This collective action creates cultural capital that is good for all.

To develop valuable cultural capital, access the informative
"Creating Cultural Impact" webinar series by becoming a member at:
www.CultureLeadershipGroup.com

Worksheet 10-1 — Meeting Stakeholders Needs

Purpose: To expand your consciousness and level of social responsibility by determining the extent to which you are meeting stakeholders' needs.

Process:

- Bring together members of your team for a group discussion.
- Assess how well you are meeting the needs of your stakeholders by completing the table below.
- After discussion about the needs, indicate the actions you want to take to improve your performance.
- Allow two to three hours for this meeting.

Stakeholder	Extent to Which Stakeholder Needs Are Being Met	Actions Which Can Be Taken to Improve Performance
Employees		
Customers		
Suppliers/Partners		
Community		

Society		
Investors		

Chapter 11

Cultural Capital
with Share of Heart

Through our own life experience and through the example of great and simple people, we awaken to the possibilities of our own lives and hearts. We glimpse the transformation that is possible through the power of our own compassion, courage, integrity, and attention.

—Jack Kornfield and Christina Feldman

Profit and Potential of Cultural Capital

The following is a case study of how one organization developed cultural capital by connecting to the hearts and minds of their stakeholders.

Case Study – Potential of Cultural Capital - Pet Industry Joint Advisory Council of Canada (PIJAC) Canada

Animal welfare is everyone's business. This is the tag line that has guided PIJAC Canada's transformation over the past two years. PIJAC Canada represents the Canadian pet industry with $6.5 billion in revenue. That is a lot of dog chow!

Two years ago the executive director of PIJAC Canada, Louis McCann, decided they needed a change in leadership and management style—in particular, the engagement and participation of board members and how the association was viewed by its stakeholders. Little did he know that what he needed was cultural transformation. What he did know for certain was that things needed to change for the board of directors (BoD) to maximize its full potential and the association to continue to grow.

Up until June 2011, the BoD would meet semi-annually for board meetings. The CEO would arrive at the planning sessions with decisions having been made, seeking approval by the BoD. Participation and engagement at the meetings were very low and most of the directors were detached from the proceedings. The CEO was not satisfied with the level of commitment or value of contributions the directors were making. While attending a conference, he happened to witness a meeting that was producing great results using professional facilitation to engage the entire room of participants. He decided to do a little research and learned about the Technology of Participation (ToP®).

Engaging a Certified ToP® Facilitator was the first step in PIJAC Canada's change process The goal was to use a participatory strategic planning process to help the BoD complete their strategic plan. The CEO admits he was quite sceptical about their possibility of success. He had been leading the BoD meetings for twenty+ years and was certain the level of engagement would not be different, even though he very much desired and needed a change.

Much to his surprise the meeting was a huge success, surpassing his hopes and expectations. Together, the group identified their challenges and opportunities, themed these into key focus areas, identified strategic objectives, created actions plans for each one for the next twelve months, and agreed on four values to guide the change process. All in eight hours.

The key ingredient that led to their success was the active participation of each board member in the whole process throughout the day. Facilitative leadership shifted control to new ways of asking questions and relating to each other so they could assume more responsibility. Helping the BoD face its challenges together let them build a clear picture of the future they wanted to create, develop strategies to achieve it, and move on to actions.

The process of being given decision-making responsibilty and the opportunity for their ideas to be heard, changed the group dynamic, as they collaborated, exchanged ideas and built a new level of trust in each other.

During the planning session, the facilitator heard limiting beliefs of how they viewed themselves based on negative stakeholder perceptions. These limiting beliefs were reducing the management team's performance and productivity. Following the planning session, an online consultative environmental scan was completed with PIJAC's key stakeholders using the drivers for change described in chapter 5.

What the stakeholders shared gave the PIJAC management team a whole new view of their world and all the untapped potential they had. Up until this point, the only voices they ever heard from were animal rights activists who hated their very existence, believing the pet industry should not make money off the backs of animals. Unfortunately, this view of the world did not take into consideration the reality that without the pet industry, where would pet owners buy food to feed their animal companions.

The new view of the world was *Animal Welfare is Everyone's Business.* Instead of portraying the purpose of the association as representing the needs of the pet industry, the new marketing message would identify their core purpose and reason for being with the love of animals. This message became their tag line to represent who they are and why they exist. It was the beginning of an inspirational journey of transformation that has continued to influence and shift mindsets, values and behaviors of all their stakeholders, and enables them daily to achieve strategic success.

Three Strategic Directions for PIJAC Canada 2012 - 2014:
1. Social Media and Communications
    Strategic Objective:
    Use social media to engage our industry and connect with our stakeholders: Facebook, Twitter, interactive websites, blogging, LinkedIn
2. Legislation
    Strategic Objective:
    To be more proactive and have better balance through efficient use of resources.

3. PIJAC Resources
Strategic Objective:
To provide a higher level of service to the membership and create more business opportunities

The four values that have transformed the cultural capital of the association and enabled PIJAC to capture a share of their stakeholders' hearts are:

- **Collaboration:** We have a commitment to respect and collaborate with our own internal and external sources for the advancement of animal well-being and the industry.
- **Excellence:** We strive continually to learn and improve so that we may help our industry achieve the highest standards possible.
- **Responsibility:** We deal honestly and fairly with our industry, the public, and one another.
- **Leadership:** PIJAC Canada is dedicated to leading the way in the development of policies, resources, and best practices that benefit pets, pet families, and Canadian pet businesses.

At the BoD level, increasing consciousness and living the four values has made the board stronger and more united in providing guidance to the association members, and kept them committed to the strategic plan. Board members are more interested in participating in roles and have taken on more responsibilities. The values have given them confidence and energy, providing valuable momentum in moving forward and making it easier to follow the plan.

Before and After Becoming a Values-Driven Organization
Before becoming a values-driven organiztion the leadership team made up their values as they went along. Leadership was taken when it was convenient. Resources were used inefficiently; the team did the work themselves instead of empowering the membership.

After deciding to become a values-driven organization, the leadership team began living the values of collaboration, leadership, and responsibility. The values have given them power and confidence when they meet stakeholders face-to-face. They are much more brazen, assertive and outgoing with traditional adversaries, putting detractors on the defensive. By living the values and seeing the results, they know they are making a difference, a result that has helped frame responses to media, stakeholders, and staff.

Cities across Canada have been equipped with a toolkit to support recommendations to City Councils. When animal issues arise, board members are sought after and quoted by the minister in press releases, raising their visibility with all stakeholders. Numerous stakeholder partnerships have been formed, promoting assistance, and looking after pets. They are recognized in communities, using partnerships to assist local community groups in giving back. A recent example: during the floods in Calgary, they helped in coordinating aid with net proceeds going to the Food Bank. Results from all this activity have increased visibility for shows, which are a major revenue generator for the association.

How did it feel as the CEO and leader going through the last two years?
It was scary to begin with, having to consult and reach out to stakeholders with whom there was a history of confrontation. Needing to "walk the talk'," be a role model, sharing decision making, and feeling responsible for staff and the whole organization. The leader often questioned himself whether he was making the right choices. This was a new journey, on a path he had not travelled before.

At first it was a struggle to get the proper level of support and involvement with staff. They had doubts and fears that took a while to address. Change and uncertainty had a way of pitting staff against each other as fear of the unknown and not having answers arose. However, through adversity comes strength and development. Overcoming the obstacles together was achieved with training in conflict resolution and change management. This training strengthened relationships and built trust as they worked collectively in solving problems.

Seeing results and unity in living the values was exciting. The association was achieving one of their main goals, retaining membership, while many other associations saw a decline in membership. The national front was getting more prominent and they were experiencing acceptance from stakeholders.

What was surprising was to see the power and impact the changes had in showcasing their work. In doing so, they received more recognition and have more active participation from stakeholders.

The leader was delighted in being able to mentor and develop staff—seeing others grow from his leadership, identifying areas of growth in staff, and empowering them to succeed.

How has the strategic plan, values and stakeholder consultations added value to the organizational development of PIJAC Canada?
PIJAC Canada is no longer seen as the big bad industry. They have changed their message to align with their true purpose and mission. This has given them power and confidence, and a broader picture of what is possible, enabling them to achieve greater results. The new orientation around values—the new social media strategies, being responsible to members, and developing the new interactive website—came at a financial cost to implement. However, stakeholders are now better informed and they are working more effectively with those who want to collaborate with them. Feedback is valued as a source of information to improve performance, instead of something to fear.

The profile of the association has been raised and they are now visible at international levels of the pet industry and outside the industry, with senior government officials. They are receiving testimonials from colleagues in Australia, England, and the Unites States. There has been a unifying effect across the association and with all its stakeholders. The new outgoing confidence has given them strength and they don't feel overwhelmed.

What is PIJAC Canada continuing to do in becoming a values-driven organization?

Networking and Sharing Resources
PIJAC Canada's foundation rests on collaboration. They value the importance of networking and the sharing of their resources with all of their industry stakeholders. They feel strongly that "Animal Welfare is Everyone's business™." This stance is reflected through their development of business partnerships that lead to a strong pet industry.

Communicating the values of a responsible pet industry to stakeholders
They believe in excellence and the importance of communicating the values of a responsible pet industry to our stakeholders. They use various tools

to communicate and celebrate their successes. They also believe in respect, developing messages that take this into account while making sure they reflect their position. They use every opportunity to promote the organization's core values in everything that they do.

Promoting the values of a responsible pet industry to the public

PIJAC Canada has an obligation to promote the values of a responsible pet industry to the public. They use every opportunity that is presented to them by media to share their point of view on matters of common interest. An engaged pet industry is the key to the enhancement of a positive pet experience.

Assuming leadership role to develop a vibrant pet industry

As stated in their mission, PIJAC Canada strives to take a leadership role in the development of a vibrant pet industry. They achieve this by insuring a leading presence at key industry events, mentoring their employees and members and by continuously developing a strong advocacy presence with legislators and decision makers.

Building a values-driven association will lead to a healthier pet industry and well-being of pets. Resources are shared and used efficiently resulting in collaboration instead of confrontation. It connects stakeholders and creates a unified voice, strengthening and supporting the mission and vision of PIJAC Canada. Promoting the values of a responsible pet industry with the public increases mindfulness of the pet experience, which strengthens the bond of existing pet owners, provides support for new pet owners, and manages the purchase impulse.

Next Steps for PIJAC Canada

PIJAC Canada will continue to create more resources to share with stakeholders and continue building media relations, advocacy, and government relations. Their goals are to promote a positive pet experience, empower retailers to reverse the declining trend in pet ownership, create a set of Best Management Practices for pet retail operations, and re-ignite fundamental values of pet ownership for:

- Mental and physical health
- Civic responsibility
- Compassionate care of animals

The PIJAC Canada case study demonstrates how it is possible to build a high performing organization and transform business results with values, ethics, and leadership. They consciously collaborated to develop a strategic plan, mapped and measured their culture, engaged stakeholders, and inspired commitment to their mission, vision and values.

Top Best 40 Companies to Work for in the USA
To demonstrate the financial returns possible between performance and engagement, refer to *Fortune Magazine's* "100 Best Companies to Work For" survey. The survey recognizes the best companies to work for in America conducted by the Great Place to Work Institute.

In the survey, two-thirds of each company's final score is based on the Institute's Trust Index survey, which is sent to a random sample of employees. The survey asks questions related to attitudes about management's credibility, job satisfaction, and the general level of camaraderie in the organization. The other third of the score is based on the company's responses to the Institute's Culture Audit, which includes detailed questions about pay and benefit programs, and a series of open-ended questions about hiring practices, internal communications, training, recognition programs, and diversity efforts.

To evaluate the financial performance of the best companies, Richard Barrett, Barrett Values Centre, measured the growth in share price of the top forty publicly traded, best companies to work for over the period of July 2002 to July 2012 and compared the result with the growth in the share price of the S&P 500[30] over the same period. The results are in figure 11-1.

---

30   S&P 500: Standard and Poor's 500, is a stock market index based on the common stock of 500 top publically traded American companies.

Figure 11-1—Top 40 Best Companies to work for in the USA

Not only did the top forty companies outperform the S&P 500, they showed more resilience in regaining their value after the economic meltdown in 2008. They regained their pre-meltdown values in just over one year, whereas the S&P 500 took three years to regain their value.

Igniting Passion and Inspiration

Companies creating conscious cultural capital by promoting a share of heart have an emotional connection to their stakeholders. This connection leads to a pattern of happy, fulfilled, creative, inspired employees who are less stressed, more productive, better at problem solving, and provide a higher quality client experience. Clients will pay extra for this kind of experience, revisiting your company, anticipating the same quality of experience. In other words this type of employee is empowered to ensure that clients will leave your company happy with the quality of service received. Customers play a particular role in this scenario as well. One of the main strategic goals of any company is to offer a product or service to the customer. Creating cultural capital and earning a share of their customer's heart translates into customer loyalty and willingness to gladly offer a share of their wallet.

This is why I enjoy going to Starbucks and pay more than I ought to for a cup of chai tea. The customer experience is enjoyable. One Friday afternoon I was waiting in a long line-up that went out the door and around the corner.

I waited because I love my Starbucks. When I got to the counter, the person in front of me had a free gift certificate for a drink. I thought to myself: "Oh that must be nice." When it was my turn the barista asked what I would like. Suddenly feeling outrageous I said I'd like what the person in front of me just had. Guess what? I got a free drink. This is employee empowerment. At that moment the barista made a loyal client for life.

Share of heart extends to producers and suppliers. Do you treat them as partners or are you constantly trying to get the most for the least? When you treat t em as partners and help them improve how they deliver their services, especially when it comes to meeting your requirements, they will become suppliers that want to give you the best products or service first. They will want to make sure you get your products when you need them—not two or three weeks late. The quality of experience you have with your suppliers can be helpful to ensure effective resource management.

Having a share of heart with community stakeholders means your community is proud to have you and will enable you to enjoy an abundant source of customers and employees. Think about your community and make sure you are doing things that are positive, socially responsible, and make a difference.

The most profitable companies are creating cultural capital with share of heart by making:

Large investments: Much like investing corporate resources in financial systems and IT systems, time and effort is invested in managing the cultural capital of the organization. For example: Southwest Airlines, the most successful airline in history, has a ninety-six-person culture committee. Imagine the kind of culture you could create with that many people creatively collaborating for the purpose of creating an inspiring workplace culture. It would be hard to fail.

WOW factor: When organizations go above and beyond in meeting the needs of their people, where the reaction from the interactions is "Wow," you've got a WOW culture. Why would you want a WOW culture? The majority of people today want "more" and they want "bigger." For this to happen there needs to be something going on that creates the WOW reaction. For example, Google has three-star chefs on staff and feeds gourmet meals to staff and visitors 24/7. When you WOW your clients, they produce higher and more frequent sales. When you WOW your employees they give you excellent performance. When you WOW your peers and treat them the way you want to be treated, you become a role model. When you WOW your superiors, you achieve promotions and raises. WOW cultures can be applied to all areas of life not just inside an organization.

Investing in your culture to build a WOW culture creates enthusiasm in the environment that increases efficiency and productivity. Teams thrive in a positive work atmosphere. This stimulates creativity and innovation. WOW cultures are a formula for employee engagement, customer satisfaction, service excellence, and high performance.

Making a Difference that is "Good for All"

Good business starts with mission, purpose and values that inspire staff to provide superior service, while increasing revenues and profits. Ongoing investment in the business creates lasting value for all stakeholders. As organizations cooperate together to create value for themselves and society, it becomes a win-win-win game for all.

PIJAC Canada's cultural transformation is based on values of leadership, collaboration, responsibility, and excellence. The focus on leadership and collaborating with all stakeholders to hear their concerns and needs, and make a difference, is giving them the sustained energy, drive, and enthusiasm to achieve and build a high performing organization.

Does business have to be a zero sum game with a winner and a loser? Does it have to be based on greed, selfishness, and exploitation?

No. Successful business is based on cooperation and voluntary exchange between investors, labor, management and suppliers, all cooperating together to create value for customers in a win-win-win game.

IBM focused on service to customers to become values-centered. They globally integrated long-term culture change over a ten-year period and increased shareholder value by $100 billion, some 84% growth. Inspiring visions are those that are not just thinking about their own company. They are thinking about all needs and levels of consciousness of different stakeholders—financial security, relationships, self-esteem, continuous learning, internal cohesion, making a difference, and service to society. When you have a vision that aspires to make a difference for all stakeholders, it creates an inclusive umbrella of good intentions that is overarching and good for all.

Creating cultural capital with share of heart that is driven by morals and ethics that are good for the whole community creates long-term, sustainable growth. Doing for others as you would want them to do for you is ethical behavior and builds trust relationships. When incorporated into sound management practices to support the efficient operations of the organization, these values provide long-term, sustainable benefits to your stakeholders. In return, employees, clients, suppliers, and your community will offer you extraordinary service. It is in the tough times that the engagement and commitment you invested in during the good times will pay off.

When creating a future vision that makes a difference and that is good for all, the alignment of strategy and culture must be good for all your stakeholders—not just your investors and shareholders, but all your stakeholders.

Figure 11-2—Stakeholder Relationship Management

So who is a stakeholder? If you think of the organization as the organs that make up the human body, one stakeholder might be the heart, another might be the lungs, another stakeholder might be the stomach and another might be the intestines. As far as the body is concerned, no one of these organs is any more or less important than the other. You need them all working together effectively and efficiently to have a healthy system. They all need to feel important and they all need to have their concerns listened to and heard. This is what is called stakeholder relationship management— SRM.

Stakeholders matter. They embody the heart, soul, and life blood of the enterprise. Being loved by your stakeholders enables you to be extraordinarily successful at creating wealth and well-being, health and performance.

In organizations with a stakeholder relationship management orientation, leaders have a disciplined dedication to the well-being of all stakeholders. For instance, suppliers are treated as partners in the decision-making process. How you manage all your stakeholders is critical to the successful functioning of the whole organization. An example, if the value of respect is a core value, stakeholders feel respected. Creating cultural capital ensures the basic needs are being met. Stakeholders feel they are treated fairly, paid enough, have healthy work relationships, autonomy, control, and competency.

Creating cultural capital with share of heart unleashes the human potential to create profitable high performance in organizations. The PIJAC Canada case study and survey of the 40 Best Companies to Work For demonstrate the power of values to drive performance and unite people in making a difference that is the good for all.

Worksheet 11-1 — Creating Cultural Capital

Purpose: To raise awareness for the value of the cultural capital and how it is created

Think of your favorite company that you love to do business with. What is it about this company that you love and keeps you going back for more?
Do you pay more their products and service? IF yes, what is it about the way they treat you and do business that you do not mind paying more?
Write a statement of the norms of behavior and values of your department.
Write a statement about the norms of behavior and values of your organization.

Describe what you think are the differences or similarities between your department and organization.

Describe what you think are differences or similarities between the company you love and your organization.

Chapter 12

Conscious Awakening

Business must view people not as a resource but as sources. A resource is a lump of coal; you use it and it's gone. A source is like the sun—virtually inexhaustible and continually generating energy, light, and warmth. There is no more powerful source of energy in the world than a turned-on, empowered human being.

—Raj Sisodia

Conscious Culture Versus Default Unconscious Culture

We have seen how to map, measure, and manage values and behaviors that engender high performance and create conscious cultural capital. Now it is time to look at unconscious default culture. We have seen how the internal employee experience is defined by the organizational culture. From the outside, the client experience is the company's brand. Who you are on the inside looks a lot like who you are on the outside. This holds true in life as well as business. An important question to ask yourself as a leader: "Do you have a conscious culture or do you have an unconscious default culture?" Are you aware of what is driving your culture and creating your brand in the market place, attracting the top talent, maximizing profit and your human potential?

Figure 12-1 – Culture and Brand

An unconscious default culture is typically the result of old-style leadership, bureaucracy, and hierarchy. It can be seen in the following values and behaviors:

- Good employees keep their heads down and do what they're asked to do without complaint.
- Good employees know how to make the boss look good.
- People who raise uncomfortable questions are troublemakers.
- People who rock the boat will pay for it; if not now, later.

- Loyalty to the boss/organization means covering up problems, truths, and even ethical issues that could make us look bad.
- Achieving individual agendas is the whole game. "There are winners and losers and I'm no loser."
- Blaming, judging, undermining others, scapegoating and other forms of "cover your ass" behavior are the norm. These behaviors involve individuals, whole teams, and entire departments.

These "fear-based" values and behaviors will not be present at all times; however, they are dysfunctional and have the effect of decreasing employee engagement, productivity, and performance. To fully "drive fear out of the workplace," it is essential for *all stakeholders* to be actively involved in rejecting these limiting values and behaviors.

"Actively rejecting" means action and personally behaving in ways that contradict these negative background beliefs.

Organizations with high levels of entropy have messengers who get shot and leaders who don't listen. Both are stereotypes reflecting our fears of one another and our need for self-protection. The courage to speak up and the courage to listen are ways to manifest change. It requires courage to "stay in the tension" of the moment, the anxiety, and particularly the fear that our sincere engagement with others might cause damage, distress, and repercussions—or that we will simply experience humiliation and anger because nothing will be done about the organizational problems we chose to bring forward. If we have two enemies in this world, it is precisely the fear of repercussions and the belief that nothing will change.

Unconscious default culture lacks the courage to stand up and consciously choose to create a different kind of workplace, one where people seek and express understanding rather than make disconnected and insensitive speeches, or hide behind one another's backs. Creating conscious culture happens only if leaders *refuse* to let fear guide their steps because fear is the essence of the old ways of behaving. Conscious culture happens only if we *choose* to address what is right in front of us.

This all works best when it is done in the name of being of service to the greater good, to one another and to our customers—being the best *for* the world, not just *in* the world.

We have all experienced and lived limiting values and behaviors. We have all contributed to negativity at one time or another, when things have gone wrong or there have been tough challenges. Here are some of the ways we *can* create a conscious culture together. To quote Mahatma Gandhi: "You must be the change you wish to see in the world."

It is essential to understand that rejecting a default culture is not the same as rejecting people.

Table 12-1 — Default versus Conscious Culture

Limiting values and behaviors of a default culture – to reject	How to create conscious culture
Blame current leaders for organizational norms but do not talk to them directly about these concerns.	Initiate conversation with current leaders about some of the limiting behaviors that are getting in the way; think together about how to mutually change things.
Blame employees for being concerned about repercussions.	Remove "fear of repercussions" as an un-discussable issue; actively make it a source of dialogue.
"Shoot the messenger" who brings forward uncomfortable issues, problems, mistakes and dilemmas. Criticize the messenger's motives.	Ask questions; embrace new information when it is uncomfortable. Thank the messenger for coming forward.
Listen to others who habitually criticize groups or individuals in another department, accepting their criticism.	Encourage and support people in turning their complaints into action steps.
Give up on people who exhibit limiting behavior, saying it won't do any good.	Talk to people about themselves and ask questions about the behaviors they exhibit.

To create a healthy conscious culture we need to become consciously competent and aware of the source and impact of the limiting behaviors and values. Only then can we begin to take ownership and responsibility for change. The learning begins with unconscious incompetence, totally unaware there is a problem. Once we are informed of the problem we move to conscious incompetence: knowing there is a problem, but not how to solve it. With dialogue and continuous learning in action learning focus groups we develop conscious competence. Once the new behaviors become ingrained we become unconsciously competent, where the behaviors are natural and automatic.

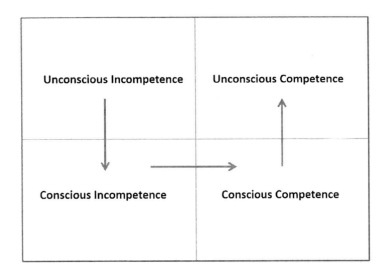

Figure 12-2—Conscious Competence Model

Between conscious and unconscious culture of old and new values and behaviors, of unconscious victimization and conscious choice, is a cultural transition of major proportions. Many organizations are undecided about which way to go and are some type of combination of both worlds. They are unsure and fear the unknown. Fear keeps people connected to traditions, tied to values that defined and created the past. It takes courage to learn and grow, to face the fears of conscious incompetence to become consciously competent. Not until a skill is mastered can we become unconsciously competent.

This learning journey can be an anxious space but also a good one for personal development. It provides the opportunity to find out who you are as a leader and what is really important to the organization for its future growth.

The following case study *Your Culture is Your Brand* from Zappos[31] is written by their CEO, Tony Hsieh. It is a great example of the experiments, innovations, and new thinking that are needed to bring positive, value-driven, high performing cultures alive.

Case Study — *Your Culture is Your Brand* – Tony Hsieh, CEO, Zappos

Building a brand today is very different from building a brand 50 years ago. It used to be that a few people got together in a room, decided what the brand positioning was going to be, and then spent a lot of money buying advertising telling people what their brand was. And if you were able to spend enough money, then you were able to build your brand.

It's a very different world today. With the Internet connecting everyone together, companies are becoming more and more transparent whether they like it or not. An unhappy customer or a disgruntled employee can blog about a bad experience with a company, and the story can spread like wildfire by email or with tools like Twitter.

The good news is that the reverse is true as well. A great experience with a company can be read by millions of people almost instantaneously.

The fundamental problem is that you can't possibly anticipate every possible touchpoint that could influence the perception of your company's brand.

For example, if you happen to meet an employee of Company X at a bar, even if the employee isn't working, how you perceive your interaction with that employee will affect how you perceive Company X, and therefore Company X's brand. It can be a positive influence, or a negative influence. Every employee can affect your company's brand, not just the front line employees that are paid to talk to your customers.

Zappos decided a long time ago that it didn't want their brand to be just about shoes, or clothing, or even online retailing. They decided to build their brand about the very best customer service and the very best customer experience. They believe that customer service shouldn't be just a department; it should be the entire company.

Advertising can only get your brand so far. If you ask most people what the "brand" of the airline industry as a whole is (not any specific airline, but the

---

31   http://blogs.zappos.com/blogs/ceo-and-coo-blog/2009/01/03/your-culture-is-your-brand

entire industry), they will usually say something about bad customer service or bad customer experience. If you ask people what their perception of the US auto industry is today, chances are the responses you get won't be in line with what the automakers project in their advertising.

So what's a company to do if you can't just buy your way into building the brand you want? What's the best way to build a brand for the long term?

In a word: culture.

At Zappos, their belief is that if you get the culture right, most of the other stuff—like great customer service, or building a great long-term brand, or passionate employees and customers—will happen naturally on its own.

They believe that your company's culture and your company's brand are really just two sides of the same coin. The brand may lag the culture at first, but eventually it will catch up.

Your culture is your brand.

So how do you build and maintain the culture that you want?

It starts with the hiring process. At Zappos, they actually do two different sets of interviews. The hiring manager and his/her team will do the standard set of interviews looking for relevant experience, technical ability, fit within the team, etc. But then their HR department does a separate set of interviews, looking purely for culture fit. Candidates have to pass both sets of interviews in order to be hired.

They've actually said no to a lot of very talented people that they know can make an immediate impact on their top or bottom line. But because they felt the people weren't culture fits, they were willing to sacrifice the short-term benefits in order to protect their culture (and therefore brand) for the long term.

After hiring, the next step to building the culture is training. Everyone that is hired into their headquarters goes through the same training that their Customer Loyalty Team (call center) reps go through, regardless of department or title. You might be an accountant, or a lawyer, or a software developer— you go through the exact same training program.

It's a four-week training program, in which they go over company history, the importance of customer service, the long term vision of the company, their philosophy about company culture—and then actually on the phone for two weeks, taking calls from customers. Again, this goes back to the belief that customer service shouldn't just be a department; it should be the entire company.

At the end of the first week of training, they make an offer to the entire class. They offer everyone $2,000 to quit (in addition to paying them for the time they've already worked), and it's a standing offer until the end of the fourth week of training. They want to make sure that employees are there for more than just a paycheck. They want employees that believe in the long term vision and want to be a part of the culture. As it turns out, on average, less than 1% of people end up taking the offer.

One of the great advantages of focusing on culture is when reporters come and visit Zappos offices. Unlike most companies, reporters are not given a small list of people they're allowed to talk to. Instead, they are encouraged to wander around and talk to whoever they want. It's the Zappos way of being as transparent as possible, which is part of their culture.

The Zappos culture can be defined in terms of ten core values:

1. Deliver WOW Through Service
2. Embrace and Drive Change
3. Create Fun and A Little Weirdness
4. Be Adventurous, Creative, and Open-Minded
5. Pursue Growth and Learning
6. Build Open and Honest Relationships With Communication
7. Build a Positive Team and Family Spirit
8. Do More With Less
9. Be Passionate and Determined
10. Be Humble

Many companies have core values, but they don't really commit to them. They usually sound more like something you'd read in a press release. Maybe you learn about them on day one of orientation, but after that it's just a meaningless plaque on the wall of the lobby.

Zappos believes that it's really important to come up with core values that you can commit to. And by commit, they mean that you're willing to hire and fire based on them. If you're willing to do that, then you're well on your way to building a company culture that is in line with the brand you want to build. You can let all of your employees be your brand ambassadors, not just the marketing or PR department. And they can be brand ambassadors both inside and outside the office.

At the end of the day, just remember that if you get the culture right, most of the other stuff—including building a great brand will fall into place on its own.

High Performance

At Zappos, measurement started before anyone was hired, with a conscious hiring process based on the core values of the company. What you measure you can manage. The toughest part about this concept is it's easy to say and hard to do. It takes a mature leader to want to measure performance and take responsibility for improving it. Leaders must to be ready and prepared to hear bad news along with the good. Unfortunately the bad news pricks the ego and hurts. You can a give person ten compliments and one criticism. What will they remember… the one criticism. In fact they will blow it up and make it ten times worse. This is nature of the mind, to focus on the negative.

Measurement is emotionally difficult. From an early age we learn to dislike performance measurement because of the negative associations connected to experiences when our performance was measured. Remember the years of report cards you brought home from school. Didn't the teacher usually say something like "John is doing well, however we know he can do better." The good seemed to come along with a negative that stole the loving praise we wanted from our parents. How challenging is it to want a positive performance appraisal knowing it will come along with perceived negative comments? Not many people enjoy performance appraisals. This extends to managers who have to prepare and deliver them.

What can turn a negative mindset towards measurement around is treating the information or criticism received as business intelligence, wisdom and ways to improve. See it as a way of setting you free to do the work that is needed. Don't look at negative comments as unconstructive rather see them as a learning opportunity to grow and develop. They are the way forward to strengthening the organization and achieving your goals. If the right light is shone on limiting behaviors, it points the way to a solution. Take the time to explore the obstacle, what it is doing to the goal, and how it is impeding your road to success. After looking at limiting factors in this way, you will see your obstacles as doorways to your future, not as blocks to performance.

One way to support continuous learning and collaboration is to ingrain the value of feedback and reflection. Make the time at the beginning and end of meetings to engage staff and find out what is happening in their world—listen and hear what people are experiencing. A leader asked me once if he should leave the room before the group reflection took place at the end of an event. He was embarrassed for me in case negative comments came up. I shared with him he could leave if he wanted; however, the comments raised would probably be the most valuable and informative to him.

Feedback, whether good or bad, is an area in which we can improve, develop, and grow. It is in the process of examining life that we become aware of the world around us. Asking questions that require self-examination and self-discovery lead to personal growth and give people a sense of gratification. This is adult education at its finest and supports transformation. It generates new awareness, connects people on deeper levels, and strengthens accountability and commitment.

Developing conscious awareness through reflection and assessment takes effort and a continuous desire to grow and learn. Conducting and debriefing a cultural values assessment sends a message to employees that you are serious about improving the organization. It provides the concrete information and data to help the organization grow and develop. Whatever is learned will give leaders valuable information on where to focus activity that will lead to the greatest amount of positive, energizing change.

Successful change happens when Leaders are 100% committed to the reasons for change. There needs to be personal alignment of the leaders' values, with the desired values of the organization, how systems and processes function, to achieve the mission and vision of the organization. This is conscious leadership. It takes skill to drive a new car watching the road ahead, the rear view mirror, listening to your passengers and the radio all at the same time. Doing this while driving is car is easy, once you know how to drive a car. Imagine you had never driven a car before, and you were put behind the wheel. It can seem scary and daunting and overwhelming to begin with, much like it did to the Executive Director of PIJAC Canada. Once the energy of living the values kicks in, the overwhelming feeling is replaced as leaders begin to experience the positive corporate life force of their values. The transformation journey gets easier with the courage and success that comes from the living the values and becoming values-driven.

When employee engagement is desired, staff are invited to participate in the assessment. This sends a powerful message to staff that they are a key ingredient in the process of growth and development. Engaging staff at all levels of the organizations in the debrief sessions increases everyone's knowledge of the work environment. From the grass roots to the top of the organization, new information is learned and shared. The engagement process empowers staff to take ownership and responsibility for the solutions that are created together. Participation is a key element is building commitment, alignment for change, and trust in management teams who are leading the change.

Participation is a powerful tool to increase engagement, ownership, and accountability. Those who participate in assessments and surveys are very curious and want to know the results. The dialogue and conversations leaders design to debrief the results can have a huge impact on transforming the culture by building ownership and responsibility for change. Facilitated conversations have the power to surface experiences, past associations, and increase awareness which can lead to new behaviors and ways of being. Staff are motivated and empowered when they are invited to participate in dialogue that will lead to change. Personal learning and development take place during these conversations. Being invited to share ideas formally is a gift they will cherish, if it is done ethically, with good intentions and actions to follow through on the suggestions and recommendations that are possible.

When leaders do not follow through on such recommendations it can have the opposite impact and create distrust and cynicism in the leadership team and the whole engagement process. Don't lead your staff up the garden path, only to let them down if you do not like the results. Good or bad, your employees want to contribute and make a difference. They are part of the problem and part of the solution. Engaging and empowering them in meaningful conversations to make meaning of the results will provide many benefits to the organization.

One of the benefits is that employees will see their leaders willing to be vulnerable. A cultural values assessment is normally done anonymously which implies people are going to speak the truth and the truth is not always pretty.

When leaders ask for information about what is happening, their intuition and inner vision is telling them to pay attention. This is the beginning of freedom. They need to accept the help from those who have the ability to give it. A leader can't do it all alone.

Common Good and Self-Interest

The aim of life is self-development. To realize one's nature perfectly, that is what each of us is here for. People are afraid of themselves, nowadays. They have forgotten the highest of all duties, the duty that one owes to one's self. Of course they are charitable. They feed the hungry, and clothe the beggar. But their own souls starve, and are naked.

—Oscar Wilde

In the context of performance, high performing individuals are those that continually learn and develop. Teams that learn and grow together are the highest performing. Organizations that are highest performing are those whose teams have perfected the art of performing together for the common good of the whole, setting aside personal self-interest.

Business people are often accused of being selfish and focused on self-interest. A common catch-phrase heard today is: Set self-interest aside and act for the "common good." Why does common good trump self-interest? What does it mean really for business?

Self-interest is an essential requirement for human survival and is needed to flourish. If we were not concerned with our well-being and the achievement of our basic human needs—food, shelter, clothing, and health, for instance—we would not be able to survive. We all need to meet our basic needs. Self-interest, however, cannot be achieved by trampling on other people. Trampling on others by violating their individual rights, for example through a fraud or a theft, is not in anyone's self-interest, no matter how lucrative the loot. Why? Because trampling on others is an invitation for them to do the same to you, and can have lasting negative repercussions.

The "common good" literally means: the sum of the good of individual members of society.

Looking again at the PIJAC Canada case study, the board of directors transformed when members were invited to set aside personal agendas and the self-interest of the companies they represented, to work together as one team for the common good of the association. In doing so they all reaped exponential benefits. Before cultural transformation, valuable resources were spent dealing with confrontation. With a common vision and shared values, members made more efficient use of their resources by collaborating and maximizing their strengths.

Self-interest can lead to competition, blame, and manipulation, while common good creates a whole that is greater than the sum of the parts. When our basic needs are met, we tend to seek more out of life. The basic needs are met for many of us in the North American society. We have a roof over our heads, food on the table, loving relationships, and access to good education. Our continuing evolution is a natural process of change and transformation as we grow and develop throughout our lives.

Our personal values as a society are not currently in alignment with business values; for example, we want to trust our leaders, and have them care about the health and welfare of others, make a difference and contribute to society as a whole. Can business as a whole say it shares the same values? If we look at our current reality, the answer is probably not. It is this misalignment that is causing disengagement leading to reduced productivity and efficiency. Business needs to find ways to create inspiring visions, meaning and purpose that align with the values of society and their employees.

Conscious awakening is happening in the world. It is no longer acceptable for businesses to avoid responsibility for all its stakeholders, even when they live on the opposite side of the planet. Thanks to social media and globalization, Third World countries will see benefit in the long term as we learn to take care of each other for the common good. It may take a pinch of enlightened self-interest and, sometimes, tragedy for change to happen; however, evolutionary transformation cannot be stopped once conscious awareness has taken place.

The following is a case study of the terrible 2013 factory fire that killed more than 1,100 workers in Bangladesh.

Bangladesh Factory Collapse:
Joe Fresh Owner Loblaws Signs Up to Safety Pact[32]

Canadian grocery giant Loblaws Companies Limited has signed a pact to improve fire and building safety in Bangladesh following the collapse of a factory in that country that killed more than 1,100 workers.

The company had items for its Joe Fresh clothing label made in the building.

As rescuers and volunteers searched for survivors among the concrete pillars and twisted rebar, shaken Loblaws executives were left to reflect on what more they might have done. "I am troubled," executive chairman Galen Weston told reporters, "that despite a clear commitment to the highest standards of ethical sourcing, our company can still be part of such an unspeakable tragedy."

"This decision reflects the company's pledge to stay in Bangladesh and underscores its firm belief that active collaboration by retail and manufacturing industries, government and non-governmental organization, is critical to driving effective and lasting change in Bangladesh," the company said in a statement.

"The accord aligns with and addresses the company's commitments to a new standard that all of its control brand products must be made in facilities that respect local construction and building codes."

The agreement requires that the companies conduct independent safety inspections, make their reports on factory conditions public, and cover the costs for needed repairs.

It also calls for them to pay up to $500,000 annually toward the effort, to stop doing business with any factory that refuses to make safety upgrades, and to allow workers and their unions to have a voice in factory safety.

The companies that agreed to the pact join two other retailers that signed the contract last year: PVH, which makes clothes under the Calvin Klein, Tommy Hilfiger, and Izod labels, and German retailer Tchibo.

Labour groups applauded the retailers that agreed to the pact, saying the agreement goes a long way toward improving working conditions in Bangladesh's garment industry, long known to be dangerous. Among them was, the United Food and Commercial Workers Canada, the country's biggest retail union.

---

32   http://www.huffingtonpost.ca/2013/05/15/bangladesh-factory-joe-fresh-loblaws-safety-pact_n_3275213.html

"On behalf of more than 250,000 UFCW Canada members—including more than 80,000 Loblaw workers—we commend Loblaw for working with UFCW and the international labour movement on this vital issue and for committing to develop and embrace a new era of life-saving health and safety standards for textile workers," national president Wayne Hanley said in a statement.

... Several other big retailers have also signed the pact including Benetton, trendy Swedish fashion chain H&M, C&A of the Netherlands, British retailers Tesco and Primark, and Spain's Inditex, owner of Zara.

... Walt Disney Co. announced that it was stopping production of its branded goods in Bangladesh. But most retailers have vowed to stay and promised to work for change.

This tragic case study demonstrates the power of collaboration between stakeholders to transform self-interest into common good, starting with several companies: coming together to assume financial responsibility for the losses and showing a desire to provide life-saving health and safety standards and respect for the local construction codes. Employees in the factories will have a voice to make a difference and contribute. With their safety reports made public, companies are going to be held accountable for repairs and adherence to the standards. This is an example of how value for human life can be uplifted when desired values and behaviors are put in place to ensure sustainable long term change that is good for all.

Common good versus self-interest is a driving force for change. As we continually evolve and change, we seek alignment with our higher selves. Success today is measured not in how we win, obtain or attain, but in how we share, grow, and become. Common good is about thriving as an organization, growing vigorously, becoming healthier and happier, and flourishing despite or because of what is happening in our external environment. It is about creating a conscious culture in the workplace with a heartbeat of excellence through shared values, ethics and leadership.

222 | CONSCIOUS CULTURE

Worksheet 12-1 — Strengthening Trust and Internal Team Cohesion

Purpose: To create a conscious team culture with a high degree of trust and communication by strengthening the internal team cohesion and ability to accomplish tasks.

Process:

- Make two large copies of the trust matrix (Figure 5.3) to be used to gather feedback from the team – one to gather strengths and one to identify areas for development

- Provide each member of the team five colored dots for strengths and a different color set of five dots for areas for development

- Ask each member to place the dots on the trust matrix identifying the strengths and areas for development of the team

- Each member should explain to the rest of the team why they have chosen to allocate the dots as they did

- Reflect on the results and begin a dialogue on how to build on the strengths and minimize the areas for development

- Ask each member to share which elements of the matrix they are least competent in and what they can do to improve

Trust Matrix Strengths	Trust Matrix Areas for Development	Proposed Actions to Improve the Level of Trust
What have we learned about our team?		

How will we hold each other accountable for making our agreed action happen?

About the Author

Joanna Barclay is a corporate leadership consultant with thirty years of experience in business transformation. From Digital Equipment to Oracle Corporation to independent consulting, she has a passion for helping leaders build high performing, values-driven workplaces.

If servant leadership is in the genes, Joanna would tend to agree based on family background and the professions she has chosen in life.

Discovering your true purpose or calling in life connects to your inner passion for living. And that is what Joanna discovered in 2000, after taking a group facilitation course with the Institute of Cultural Affairs. As a result she changed professional careers and became a Certified Professional Facilitator. In 2010 she was introduced to the Barrett Values Centre and since then has been a Cultural Transformation Tools Consultant, empowering leaders to be the change they want to see.

Now, every time she facilitates or speaks it's in the role of servant leadership, helping leaders create a culture of participation by developing collaborative connections, increasing team synergy, and building consensus. Working with leadership teams and being a facilitative leader gives her the opportunity to further change by the people, for the people, and help them reach their true potential.

With extensive experience in information management and management consulting, Joanna has expertise in leadership development, public speaking, facilitating organizational culture change, strategic planning, designing and leading training seminars.

Joanna has worked with a wide variety of clients including federal and municipal government departments, private corporations, associations, and non-profits. She also has years of business analysis, application development, and sales experience with major IT companies.

In her work with teams and leaders Joanna has gained deep insight into the human dynamics of effective relationships and communication. She is Canadian director of the TLEX Program (Transformational Leadership for Excellence), a gold standard in leadership development that enables individuals and organizations to reach their full potential. The program is delivered by the International Association for Human Values, a global, non-profit, humanitarian organization.

Joanna is married with three children. A loving wife and mother, she counts this as the most meaningful of all roles in her life and a constant source of love, inspiration and growth.

To schedule Joanna Barclay for a speaking event,
consulting, or leadership development seminar visit:
www.CultureLeadershipGroup.com/contactus

Annex – Now What?

Implementing a Framework for Change

Leaders aspiring to build a high-performing organization will benefit by having a framework to guide transformation efforts. For culture change projects to be successful, four-way alignment is required to change the whole organization. This is called whole-system change. It is achieved by aligning four areas: personal alignment, values alignment, mission alignment, and structure alignment.

Four conditions must be met for whole-system change to occur. These are:

1. *Personal alignment*: There must be an alignment between the values and beliefs of individuals, and their words, actions and behaviors. This is particularly important for the leadership group. It is important that leaders are authentic and walk their talk— Authenticity.

2. *Structural alignment*: There must be an alignment between the stated values of the organization, and the behaviors of the organization as they are reflected in the structures, systems, processes, policies, incentives and procedures of the organisation. It is important that the values are institutionalised— Integrity.

3. *Values alignment*: There must be an alignment between the personal values of employees and the stated values of the organization. It is

227

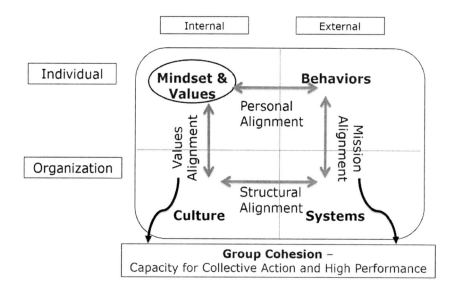

Figure Annex-1 — Whole-System Change – Four-Way Alignment

important that all employees feel at home in the organization and can bring their whole selves to work.

4. *Mission alignment*: There must be an alignment between sense of motivation and purpose of all employees, and the mission and vision of the organization. It is important that every employee, manager and leader has a clear line of sight between the work they do each day and the mission or vision of the organization, so they know how they make a difference.

Values alignment and mission alignment together create group cohesion. Engineering parallel shifts in all four quadrants at the same time is called **whole-system change.**

When the action and behaviors of the individual and groups are in alignment with the values and behaviors that they tell us they espouse, we consider this person or group to operate with authenticity and integrity.

Individual and collective values and behaviors shape the culture of an organization. Conducting a Cultural Values Assessment (CVA) with key stakeholders will provide the organization valuable information on the current and desired values and behaviors of its people.

For whole-system change to occur there must be a parallel shift in personal alignment, structural alignment, values alignment and mission alignment. All four relationships must change in the same direction for the group to experience a shift in consciousness.

The way to bring about such a change in an organization is through workshops, seminars and training programs that focus on personal alignment and group cohesion (values alignment and mission alignment), and structural alignment—changes in rules, regulations, systems and processes, and structures of governance that reflect the values and behaviors of the new level of consciousness.

The personal alignment and group cohesion programs should be tailored to correspond to the levels of consciousness of the group. The Seven Levels of Consciousness Model provides the necessary insights to design such programs. The CVA survey tells you exactly where the group is and where it wants to go in terms of values and levels of consciousness. These understandings are particularly important in choosing the implementation methodologies that are appropriate for the personal alignment and group cohesion programs.

Common Mistakes

Mistakes are often made in cultural transformation because the interdependencies between all four quadrants are not well understood.

Mistake 1: Focus only on personal alignment.

Many organizations focus on personal alignment without doing anything about structural alignment. This serves only to aggravate the situation. Managers and employees who have experienced a personal alignment program shift to a higher level of consciousness while policies and procedures in the organization still reflect the old level of consciousness.

Mistake 2: Focus only on group cohesion.

Another mistake is focusing on structural change without carrying out personal alignment. This limits the potential of success for group cohesion because people enter these programs without self-understanding or strong interpersonal skills. It would be better for people to enter the change programs having already experienced a shift in consciousness.

Therefore, for maximum impact, personal alignment should precede group cohesion and structural alignment should follow personal alignment or be carried out in parallel. When this happens, organizations can shift smoothly to a new level of consciousness.

Whole-system change is divided into two phases:
- Phase 1: Preparation and
- Phase 2: Implementation.

The preparation phase begins with leadership commitment to building an engagement plan to map and measure the current and desired culture of the organization. It culminates in the definition of a strategy for the implementation of a whole system change program, core values, and the key performance indicators that will be used to measure the success of the program.

The implementation phase includes the interventions and programs required to benefit its people on the journey to attain exceptional high performance.

For a free e-book on the 9 Steps to Building
a High Performing Workplace visit:
www.CultureLeadershipGroup.com

Whole-System Change—Preparation Phase

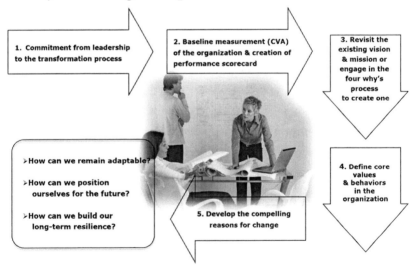

Figure Annex-2— Whole-System Change Preparation Phase

Step 1 – Leadership Commitment:
- Develop a business case for change:
  - o Environmental scan
  - o Discovery interviews with key stakeholders
  - o Feedback session with leadership team
- Map values and behaviors of leadership group by conducting a Small Group Values Assessment
  - o Debrief values assessment
- Connect, align, and build trust on leadership team
- Create and share a compelling change story—WHY do we need to change?

Step 2 – Baseline Measurement— Cultural Values Assessment:
- Conduct a Cultural Values Assessment of whole organization
- Include demographics such as:
  - o Position
  - o Business unit
- Debrief results with teams
- Identify opportunities and obstacles to cultural change
- Provides guidance in the development of programs for:
  - o Personal alignment
  - o Group cohesion
  - o Structural alignment
- Identify key performance indicators for values management such as building trust and leadership development

Step 3 – Revisit Mission and Vision:
- Gives direction to the change process
- Identify the core motivations of the leadership group
- Define and develop agreement on the core business of the organization
- Revisit mission and vision statements
  - o Ensure they are still relevant and inspiring to the leadership group, managers and staff
- Create an internal mission of how the organization is going to grow and develop internally
- Create an internal vision of what the organization will look like in five to ten years

- Create an external mission of what the organization does for its customers
- Create an external vision of the impact the organization wants to have on society

Step 4 – Define Core Values and Behaviors:

- Select values that will:
  - o Provide guidelines for acceptable and unacceptable behaviors
  - o Support the organization in creating the future it wants to experience
  - o Provide direction in decision making
- Identify the behaviors that support the chosen values
- Write behavior statements in a way that can be used in a performance monitoring process

Step 5 – Develop Compelling Reasons for Change:

- The compelling reasons for change position the company to take advantage of future opportunities and build long-term resilience and sustainability
- The results of the cultural values assessment provide significant input into the compelling reasons for change
- The purpose is to unite everyone behind the whole-system change process
- Reasons must be grounded in reality and driven by realistic optimism for a better future

Whole-System Change—Implementation Phase

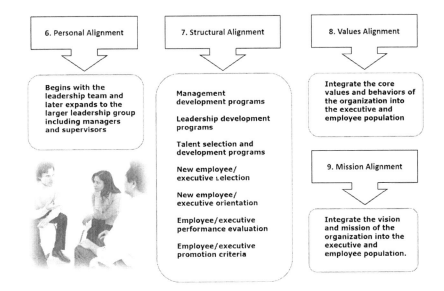

Figure Annex-3 — Whole-System Change Implementation Phase

Step 6 – Personal Alignment

Personal awareness and alignment programs to support self-mastery:

- TLEX Program—Transformational Leadership for Excellence
- Leadership Values Assessment
  - o Assessment of strengths, and areas of development
- Leadership Development Report
  - o Assessment based on twenty-six competencies
- Mindset and behavior transformation workshop
- Relationship Awareness training

Step 7 – Systems and Procedures Alignment:

- Reconfigure systems and processes to align with the vision, mission, values and behaviors of the organization
- These processes form the underlying formal and informal behavioral reward systems that support culture and materialize "how things are done around here"
- Systems that may need to be reconfigured:
  - o Management development programs

 o Leadership development programs
 o Talent selection and development programs
 o New employee/executive selection
 o New employee/executive orientation
 o Employee/executive performance evaluation
 o Employee/executive promotion criteria

Step 8 – Values Alignment:

- Communicate the compelling reasons for change
- Outline the vision, mission, values and behaviors
- Align personal values with organizational values
- Empower employees to bring the best of themselves to work

Step 9 – Mission Alignment:

- Integrate the vision and mission of the organization into the executive and employee population
- Ensure there is a strong link between employees' sense of purpose or mission and the collective sense of purpose for the organization
- Communication of objectives that define and clarify the mission focus and channel employee energies in the same direction

Individual Values Assessment—Cultural Transformation Coaching

How aligned are you with the culture and values of your organization? How well do you connect with your organization and the work you do? Do you think the organization is on the right track? All these questions and more are answered with an Individual Values Assessment (IVA).

Investing in an Individual Values Assessment (IVA) provides time for reflection to examine personal and organizational values at work.

A surprise for leaders who take the IVA is how a quick and easy process like answering three questions can provide so much insight into the functioning of an organization. The coaching session that accompanies an IVA identifies the alignment between personal and organizational values and how misalignment affects a person. It shows what is having a negative impact and reducing individual performance, and follows with the steps that will have a positive effect of increasing personal and organizational levels of engagement, performance, and competitive advantage.

The IVA is particularly valuable in how it makes leaders consider how they do things and—because people tend to be task oriented—how personal values are often taken for granted, not put at the forefront. Leaders who do the IVA learn a lot about how to measure values and behaviors, making the intangible nature of culture more tangible.

A personal IVA coaching session helps leaders to think about things they could be doing to achieve a desired culture. The data does not lie. It gives leaders a benchmark of where they are now and where they want to be down the road; with measurement, what was once a struggle becomes much easier for leaders to manage.

The IVA process identifies key values not consciously thought of before. It provides a framework to look at the entire values system, to recognize the organization's strengths and areas of entropy or limiting values. It shows in a tangible way what a person is feeling about the organization, what is working for and against, what is energizing, and what is demotivating, frustrating, and causing disengagement.

"The Individual Values Assessment (IVA) I conducted with Joanna from the Barrett Values Centre was like getting an MRI for our organization. It allowed a very specific and deep-dive into the root causes of performance gaps and opportunities. Most importantly, it led to very progressive and positive changes in performance."

Robert Francis Seguin, Managing Partner,
The Productive Leadership Institute

Reflect and explore your organization's performance gaps and opportunities with an Individual Values Assessment. Visit
www.CultureLeadershipGroup.com/iva

Benefits
- The IVA deepens your understanding of what is important to you in your life and what changes are necessary for you to find personal fulfillment in your organization.

- The IVA provides insights into how well aligned you are with the culture of your organization.

Key Attributes

- **Expert Evaluation**— The IVA evaluates how aligned you are with your organization.
- **Fast Turnaround**— An IVA data report can be delivered upon the completion of the online assessment.
- **Multiple Languages**— The online survey and plots are available in multiple languages.

Languages for IVA Online Survey and Data Report		
• Afrikaans	• French Canadian	• Norwegian
• Arabic	• German	• Polish
• Brazilian	• Greek	• Portuguese
• Chinese	• Hindi	• Romanian
• Czech	• Hungarian	• Russian
• Danish	• Icelandic	• Slovakian
• Dutch	• Indonesian	• Spanish
• English	• Italian	• Swedish
• Estonian	• Korean	• Tamil
• Finnish	• Latvian	• Thai
• Flemish	• Lithuanian	• Turkish
• French	• Malay	• Vietnamese
		• Xhosa

Transformational Leadership Development

Today's leaders must be transformative and adaptive, in other words, facilitative. You are called on for more than superficial solutions to problems. You transform whole systems, leveraging strengths to address root issues, aligning the intentions of individuals and entire organizations, and operate from an empowering paradigm. The transformational leader engages and motivates people through difficult times, opens up space for authentic dialogue, and clarifies the group's wisdom in forging solutions and implementing change.

Increase your ability to:

- Generate creativity in the entire group
- Engage and empower the people around you
- Implement plans and initiatives more effectively
- Increase commitment to plans and their implementation

Recommended Courses: www.CultureLeadershipGroup.com/leadershipskills

The Technology of Participation (ToP®)— Group Facilitation Training
Meetings That Work

In today's world of truncated timelines, increased workloads, and demands for workplace democracy, we need group decisions made quickly, positively, and with diminished frustration. We also need to ensure that meetings are effective, efficient, and highly productive. This course is designed for the person who needs tools to enhance participation and productivity in various types of meetings.

Learn how to:

- Increase the productivity of the group
- Focus the purpose and intent of large and small meetings
- Aid the group in its decision-making processes
- Handle difficult situations in groups
- Match process tools to each group's needs

Group Facilitation Methods

Move beyond "seat-of-the-pants" facilitation and reliance on instinct, to use the most powerful facilitation methods and processes available. Learn step-by-step approaches to clear thinking, sound decisions, solid consensus, and open dialogue. Learn how to:

- Facilitate groups more effectively
- Make meetings more productive and efficient
- Focus a diverse group's energy on common goals
- Create a sense of teamwork and improve staff morale
- Tap into group creativity to maximize productivity

Learn the Focused Conversation Method, which provides a structure for clear dialogue and reflection; probes beneath the surface to the depth of a topic; encourages a diversity of perspectives; and leads to decisions. Learn the Consensus Workshop Method to engage participation of diverse group members and create genuine consensus. Build effective team partnerships and lead large groups effectively.

Facilitated Planning

Executives, managers, and consultants must maximize a group's potential to think and act strategically and find effective solutions to challenges. This course demonstrates practical techniques to get the synthesis of strategic thinking into the analysis of strategic planning. The ToP® participatory planning process achieves consensus among participants with diverse economic, political, and cultural perspectives. If you want real vision rather than the manipulation of numbers, and real action and results instead of paper plans that gather dust, this course is a must. Learn how to:

- Create an inspiring and inclusive vision everyone wants
- Safely identify hidden, underlying issues, and systemic blockages
- Shape innovative strategy with group commitment
- Generate practical action plans empowering immediate and effective implementation
- Link vision and action to mission, mandate, and values

International Association of Facilitators (IAF)—

Core Competencies for Certification
The field of facilitation and facilitative leadership competencies are increasingly viewed as key organizational components, without which organizations and teams are not able to perform to their full potential. Through the certification designation, the IAF provides a path to educate and develop skills that enable the organization to perform at above-average expectations.

The question asked most often is "What is a professional facilitator?"

Below are competencies that help to build a culture of participation to attract, engage, and retain your top performers, and become a high performing organization.

A. Create Collaborative Client Relationships
B. Plan Appropriate Group Processes
C. Create and Sustain a Participatory Environment
D. Guide Group to Appropriate and Useful Outcomes
E. Build and Maintain Professional Knowledge
F. Model Positive Professional Attitude

A. Create Collaborative Client Relationships
1. Develop working partnerships
- Clarify mutual commitment
- Develop consensus on tasks, deliverables, roles & responsibilities
- Demonstrate collaborative values and processes such as in co-facilitation

2. Design and customize applications to meet client needs
- Analyze organizational environment
- Diagnose client need
- Create appropriate designs to achieve intended outcomes
- Predefine a quality product & outcomes with client

3. Manage multi-session events effectively
- Contract with client for scope and deliverables
- Develop event plan

- Deliver event successfully
- Assess / evaluate client satisfaction at all stages of the event or project

B. Plan Appropriate Group Processes

1. Select clear methods and processes that

- Foster open participation with respect for client culture, norms, and participant diversity
- Engage the participation of those with varied learning / thinking styles
- Achieve a high quality product / outcome that meets the client needs

2. Prepare time and space to support group process

- Arrange physical space to support the purpose of the meeting
- Plan effective use of time
- Provide effective atmosphere and drama for sessions

C. Create and Sustain a Participatory Environment

1. Demonstrate effective participatory and interpersonal communication skills

- Apply a variety of participatory processes
- Demonstrate effective verbal communication skills
- Develop rapport with participants
- Practice active listening
- Demonstrate ability to observe and provide feedback to participants

2. Honor and recognize diversity, ensuring inclusiveness

- Encourage positive regard for the experience and perception of all participants
- Create a climate of safety and trust
- Create opportunities for participants to benefit from the diversity of the group
- Cultivate cultural awareness and sensitivity

3. Manage group conflict

- Help individuals identify and review underlying assumptions
- Recognize conflict and its role within group learning / maturity
- Provide a safe environment for conflict to surface
- Manage disruptive group behavior

- Support the group through resolution of conflict

4. Evoke group creativity
- Draw out participants of all learning and thinking styles
- Encourage creative thinking
- Accept all ideas
- Use approaches that best fit needs and abilities of the group
- Stimulate and tap group energy

D. Guide Group to Appropriate and Useful Outcomes

1. Guide the group with clear methods and processes
- Establish clear context for the session
- Actively listen, question, and summarize to elicit the sense of the group
- Recognize tangents and redirect to the task
- Manage small and large group process

2. Facilitate group self-awareness about its task
- Vary the pace of activities according to needs of group
- Identify information the group needs, and draw out data and insight from the group
- Help the group synthesize patterns, trends, root causes, frameworks for action
- Assist the group in reflection on its experience

3. Guide the group to consensus and desired outcomes
- Use a variety of approaches to achieve group consensus
- Use a variety of approaches to meet group objectives
- Adapt processes to changing situations and needs of the group
- Assess and communicate group progress
- Foster task completion

E. Build and Maintain Professional Knowledge

1. Maintain a base of knowledge
- Knowledgeable in management, organizational systems and development, group development, psychology, and conflict resolution
- Understand dynamics of change
- Understand learning and thinking theory

2. Know a range of facilitation methods
- Understand problem solving and decision-making models
- Understand a variety of group methods and techniques
- Know consequences of misuse of group methods
- Distinguish process from task and content
- Learn new processes, methods, & models in support of client's changing/ emerging needs

3. Maintain professional standing
- Engage in ongoing study / learning related to the field of facilitation
- Continuously gain awareness of new information in the profession of facilitation
- Practice reflection and learning
- Build personal industry knowledge and networks
- Maintain certification

F. Model Positive Professional Attitude

1. Practice self-assessment and self-awareness
- Reflect on behavior and results
- Maintain congruence between actions and personal and professional values
- Modify personal behavior / style to reflect the needs of the group
- Cultivate understanding of one's own values and their potential impact on work with clients

2. Act with integrity
- Demonstrate a belief in the group and its possibilities
- Approach situations with authenticity and a positive attitude
- Describe situations as facilitator sees them and inquire into different views
- Model professional boundaries and ethics (as described in ethics and values statement)

3. Trust group potential and model neutrality
- Honor the wisdom of the group
- Encourage trust in the capacity and experience of others
- Vigilant to minimize influence on group outcomes

- Maintain an objective, non-defensive, non-judgmental stance
- For more information and resources on facilitation competencies visit www.iaf-world.org

Facilitative Leadership Tips

Anyone can adopt a style of facilitation without loss of authority, respect and integrity, regardless of one's current role as leader, manager, supervisor, or employee. This style can be used to unblock and promote continuous learning.

For innovative, inclusive facilitation tools and techniques to support your team's development become a member at: www.CultureLeadershipGroup.com

A facilitative style can be consciously nurtured by making shifts like the ones listed below.

From. . .	. . . To
Telling and directing	Asking questions
Vague big questions	Several specific questions
Getting a particular decision	Thinking clearly to create a wise decision
Summarizing	Reflecting
Right and wrong answers	Learning from every experience
Debate	Dialogue
Arguing about competing opinions	Understanding the values beneath the opinions
One answer	Sets of related answers
Finding Problems	Finding meaning, root causes, and insight
Entrenched position is a problem	Entrenched positions indicate past insight and wisdom
Analysis	Balancing synthesis with analysis
Reducing problem to understand it	Pulling analysis together into shared understanding

Emotions are unprofessional	Emotions are indicators of deep concern
Categorizing	Configuring
Using existing distinctions to sort diversity	Uncovering insight, connections and creativity
Recognizing personal biases	Honoring diverse perspectives
Group dynamics is a problem to be solved	Diversity is an asset
Giving up and compromising	Creating an inclusive solution
Consensus as agreement	Consensus as ability to more forward together

Relationship Awareness Training

Improve Relationships and Manage Conflict

Working together productively doesn't come naturally to everyone. Have you ever observed or experienced a situation where organizational effectiveness in the workplace suffered because of differences among individuals? This challenge is all too common as differing work styles and conflict can lead to reduced efficiency and increased employee absenteeism and turnover. In today's business environment, effective interpersonal relationships are essential to a healthy workplace.

Fortunately, there are ways to improve interactions among individuals to support organizational transformation and leadership development. The quality of the relationships among members of an organization can have an impact on its performance: people collaborate more effectively when they understand themselves and others better, and when they recognize and value each other's strengths.

The Strength Deployment Inventory (SDI©) is a suite of tools based on Relationship Awareness®. It consists of a series of instruments that focus on emphasizing people's strengths, and suggests how those strengths may be used to improve work relationships. Whether you need to manage talent to attract, engage or retain the best or want to build leadership skills for better work relationships, the SDI® suite of tools can meet your business needs. Alone or in combination with other Relationship Awareness tools, the SDI® builds self-awareness and openness to diversity, and enhances participants' ability to communicate effectively and to deal with conflict productively.

The SDI® can be helpful in numerous contexts including: enterprise renewal, talent management, leadership development, conflict resolution, change management, assessment of organizational culture, coaching, communication skills development, project management, and team building. It is available in French and in English.

For your personal SDI® visit: www.CultureLeadershipGroup.com/sdi

For Individuals and Teams
The SDI® tool is a personal development tool that can help you:
• Increase self-awareness
• Understand what motivates you
• Identify your strengths
• Understand yourself and others better
• Improve how you deal with conflict

For Managers
The SDI® has been used successfully by many organizations to:
• Manage talent successfully
• Build stronger teams and leaders
• Create a healthy work environment
• Increase performance for better results
• Transform conflict

The Organizational Journey

Cultural transformation happens within the context of organizational transformation and as a result of strategic planning. This is often when new initiatives are developed that require a change in employee behavior and/or the way systems and processes perform. Leaders and management see the need to develop and grow the organization to meet the needs of employees, clients, and the marketplace.

The organizational journey map[33] is a useful tool for seeing where the organization is currently and where it wishes to grow. The leadership and skills segments of the map are particularly helpful in understanding what new training and development is necessary to develop the skills needed to lead cultural change. As the saying goes, "leaders need to be the change they wish

---

33   Reference: Edges Article & ICA Associates Organizational Transformation Training

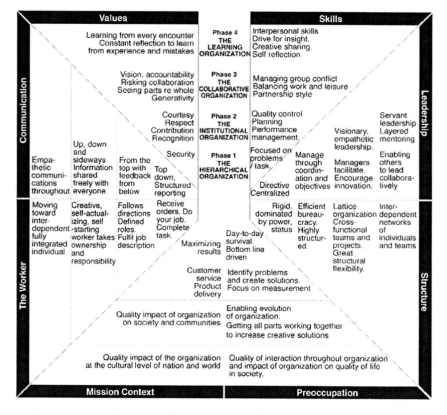

**Figure Annex-4—Map of the Journey of Organizational Development
Reference: ©The Canadian Institute of Cultural Affairs, 2005**

to see." This implies leaders need to have the competencies for managers and employees to follow.

The *Organizational Journey Map* was developed by ICA Associates using the work of Harrison Owen, Willis Harman, Brian Hall, and some ICA offices. The map is made up of two images superimposed on each other:

- eight segments of an organization
  - o skills
  - o leadership
  - o structure
  - o preoccupation
  - o mission context
  - o the worker

o communication
o values
• four phases of levels of development
  o the hierarchical organization
  o the institutional organization
  o the collaborative organization
  o the learning organization

There is no good or bad place for an organization to be on the map. What is helpful is to know what you are and where you want to be. Then you can plan the journey.

The map is also a helpful tool when people see themselves at different places on it—it can then be the catalyst for conversation that builds understanding of the current situation and how a group wants to develop.

Possible Uses for the Organizational Journey Map
• Diagnosing collective problems
• Setting a context for visioning
• Articulating a board or senior executive leadership perspective
• Dialogue during a time of structural uncertainty
• Exposing contradictory values and assumptions that undermine progress

The Organizational Journey

Transforming an organization means changing the whole network of interrelated and inter-dependent relationships—a process that has been called "whole-system change." A first step in this change process is to understand the make-up of the organization's current world view. Discussions on the *current values* that are selected in the Barrett Values Centre (BVC) Cultural Values Assessment (CVA) described in chapter 8 are helpful in this process. For transformation to occur, the organization must then develop consensus and choose a new desired paradigm. The *desired values* from the BVC CVA are helpful and provide a roadmap for guiding these conversations. When there is a desired shift in the image of the organization, the priority values shift. It is not simply the focus, structure, and leadership of the organization that change, but the core values, skills, and operating style.

To choose a new operating paradigm and mindset, the organization needs a vision. It needs an image not just of greater size or profitability, but of higher maturity and fulfillment. It also needs a way to see where it is stuck now, and an overview of the whole journey of possible development.

Phase 1 The Hierarchical Organization

Leadership in the hierarchical organization operates as benevolent paternalism. Orders and incentives come from the top down. Management may believe in spending time listening to what subordinates say, but this feedback is commonly ignored in the real process of management. The worker is seen as a child tended by a fatherly leader; by following the rules and working hard, he or she can win favor in the organization. The top-rated skills involve problem-solving, administrative effectiveness, and "keeping calm." Basically, this style is reactive. The main agenda is responding to problems and crises as they occur. A major preoccupation of management is keeping labor submissive, which may involve discouraging unions. Overly zealous accountability means the workforce sees keeping and looking busy as a prime value.

Phase 2 The Institutional Organization

This is the large, efficient bureaucracy. Its style is that of responsiveness. It is preoccupied with customer service. Communication is from the top, but informed by feedback from below. The mode is task-oriented and output-focused. This is the kingdom of the team, quality control, and management by objectives. Loyal subordinates know their functions, but often find themselves acting out the same scripts for every performance. The gift of the institutional organization is great order, great predictability, and great loyalty to staff and to customers. The responsiveness to clients is rapid; responsiveness to social change is glacial.

The shift from an institutional style (phase 2) to a collaborative style (phase 3) really involves a whole-system transition that only happens over time.

Phase 3 The Collaborative Organization

The first two phases are preoccupied with the patterns of power relations, profit, efficient production and customer service. If these two phases are all about structure, the last two are more about process, although structure remains important.

Interaction is the core characteristic of the collaborative phase. Organizations in this phase aim for real teamwork between all members and departments. Their mission and goal is to make a quality impact on society. Structurally, this is a lattice organization. All the parts are integral to the whole, and no part may be replaced without altering the whole. Such organizations are concerned about reducing rigidity, and increasing the flow of creativity.

This type of organization has great structural flexibility. The leadership is enthusiastic, visionary, and empathetic. Their management style is facilitative. Key skills at this level are delegating responsibility, managing group conflict, balancing work with leisure; growing from experience, and helping others do the same. The main difference between collaborative and lower-phase organizations is the free flow of ideas. Management is more concerned about stimulating creativity than preventing unauthorized action. Communication is up, down, and sideways. People talk about how to make the institution more humane. Staff self-actualize and seek to serve society through their work.

The gifts of this situation are obvious: synergy and alignment between the parts of the organization, and a mission related to social service. The danger occurs when the organization begins to see itself as one big happy family and staff trust and enjoy one another too much to really hold each other accountable.

Phase 4 The Learning Organization

The learning organization is blessed with a high degree of interactive learning, an emphasis on human resource development, and concern with "making a difference." To some extent, the organization itself becomes a message to the world, offering its own vision of human relations for the future. This phase involves a new take on "quality" and "learning." The learning organization is a network of self-directed teams. Using the model of servant leadership, the leader enable others to maximize their performance through a system of layered mentoring. The quality of communication is empathetic throughout. The worker is a microcosm of the organization, and is encouraged to assume responsibility for the whole, beyond his or her job description. Outside involvement in the community and personal growth are encouraged as relevant to the organization's vision.

In such a team, every encounter is regarded as a learning situation. Interpersonal and reflective skills for gaining insight are crucial. A core set of values is built or changed by consensus. A superb flexibility enables the organization to deal with rapid change.

Unlike the single-minded focus on a bottom line, or the single program of a silver bullet, this vision of quality involves balance. The organization works to perfect a juggling act, honoring the needs of the person, the group, and the greater community. The danger at this phase is a collapse of structure in favor of "networking." It is more difficult to create consensus with a limited structure. Accountability can slip, and with it, quality work.

Mistakes and Tips

1. On viewing the organizational journey map, some managers mistakenly assume it is possible to shift directly to another level. It is never so clear-cut. Organizations cannot make such neatly defined changes overnight. What is feasible is for a few people to share a vision, and prefigure a future style in their own work. Such an example of a better way can gradually shift how the whole group does things.

2. Since some people will always respond to change faster than others, the organization is bound to be spread over two or more phases. The map is, therefore, not meant to be used as a static model. Organizations tend to evolve more in some arenas than others. A team will be at different stages in different areas, and at different times

3. It stands to reason that if the leadership is not at least a stage ahead of others in the organization, there is not much real possibility for development. Somebody has to be ahead of the game. However, leadership understandings and values may be ahead of their skills. As an organization begins to push into a new phase, images and understandings may change rapidly, but the skills that belong to that phase still take time to develop. Only after the new skills are mastered can the organization begin to live and operate on a higher level.

4. The order of stages in this model makes it clear that a hierarchical organization doesn't have much chance of changing directly into a learning organization.

To view an informative webinar on how to utilize the
Organizational Journey Map, and help you transform your
organization into a high performing workplace become a member at:
www.CultureLeadershipGroup.com

Worksheet Annex 1-4— Organizational Assessment

Purpose: To understand the current reality of the organization, how it is operating, and how it wishes to grow, develop and transform using the Organizational Journey Map.

Describe the current reality: Individually assess the organization using a worksheet version of the organizational journey map. In small groups help each other clarify understanding (it's not about agreement) Place one color of dots in each of the eight segments for where the organization is right now.
The whole group looks and discusses the resulting image. What was behind your thinking in placing the dots where you did?

Place a second color dot in each of the eight segments to describe the kind of organization you want it to be in the future.
The whole group looks and discusses the resulting image.
What was behind your thinking in placing the dots where you did?

What is the shift in values for each segment?
What is each shift telling you?
What behaviors are needed to demonstrate the specific shift in values?

What would indicate the organization is ready for each shift?
What parts of the organization are already operating from the desired future?

What are the issues, constraints, blocks, contradictions, problems, or behaviors that could stop you from making the shift?

What actions are needed to enable you to carry out the developmental shift in values and behaviors?

Bibliography

Anderson, Dean, Linda Ackerman Anderson. *Beyond Change Management: How to Achieve Breakthrough Results Through Conscious Change Leadership.* San Francisco: Pfeiffer, 2010.

Barrett, Richard. *Liberating the Corporate Soul: Building a Visionary Organization.* Woburn, MA: Butterworth-Heinemann, 1988.

Barrett, Richard. *Building a Values-Driven Organization: A Whole System Approach to Cultural Transformation.* Woburn, MA: Butterworth-Heinemann, 2006.

Barrett, Richard. *The New Leadership Paradigm: Leading Self Leading Others Leading an Organization Leading in Society.* http://valuescentre.com, 2010.

Barrett, Richard. *The Values-Driven Organization: Unleashing Human Potential for Performance and Profit.* New York: Routledge, 2014.

Heider, John. *The Tao of Leadership: Lao Tzu's Tao Te Ching Adapted for a New Age.* Atlanta, GA: Humanics New Age, 1997.

Johnson, Judy, Les Dakens, Peter Edwards, Ned Morse. *Switchpoints: Culture Change on the Fast Track to Business Success.* New Jersey: John Wiley & Sons Inc., 2008.

Kraemer, Harry M. Jansen Jr., *From Values to Action: The Four Principles of Values-Based Leadership.* San Francisco: Josey-Bass, 2011.

Rhodes, Ann, Nancy Shepherdson. *Built on Values: creating an enviable culture that outperforms the competition.* San Francisco: Josey-Bass, 2011.

Sisodia, Raj, John Mackey. *Conscious Capitalism: Liberating the Corporate Spirit.* Boston: Harvard Business School Publishing Corporation, 2013.

Sisodia, Raj, Jag Sheth, David B. Wolfe. *Firms of Endearment: How World Class Companies Profit from Passion and Purpose.* New Jersey: Prentice Hall Publishing, 2007.

Stanfield, Brian R., *The Art of Focused Conversation: 100 Ways to Access Group Wisdom in the Workplace.* A ToP® Method of the Institute of Cultural Affairs, Gabriola Island: New Society Publishers, 2000.

Staples, Bill. *Transformational Strategy: Facilitation of ToP® Paticipatory Planning.* Bloomington, IN: INUniverse, 2013.

Weins, Ron. *Building Organizations that Leap Tall Buildings in a Single Bound.* Ottawa, 2012.

Wheatley, Margaret. *Leadership and the New Science: Discovering Order in a Chaotic World.* San Francisco: Berrett-Koehler, 1999.

Whitmore, Diana. *Psychosynthesis Counselling in Action.* London: Sage Publications, 2000.

Whitmore, John. *Coaching for Performance.* London: Nicholas Brealey, 2009.

Wilson, Priscilla H., *The Facilitative Way: Leadership That Makes a Difference.* Shawnee Mission: Team Tech Press, 2003.

CPSIA information can be obtained at www.ICGtesting.com
Printed in the USA
BVOW05*0918011014

369076BV00003B/14/P

9 781630 471552